Series/Number 07-102

TYPOLOGIES AND TAXONOMIES
An Introduction to Classification Techniques

KENNETH D. BAILEY
University of California, Los Angeles

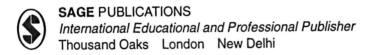

SAGE PUBLICATIONS
International Educational and Professional Publisher
Thousand Oaks   London   New Delhi

For information address:

 SAGE Publications, Inc.
2455 Teller Road
Thousand Oaks, California 91320

SAGE Publications Ltd.
6 Bonhill Street
London EC2A 4PU
United Kingdom

SAGE Publications India Pvt. Ltd.
M-32 Market
Greater Kailash I
New Delhi 110 048 India

Printed in the United States of America

Library of Congress Catalog Card No. 89-043409

Bailey, Kenneth D.
    Typologies and taxonomies: An introduction to classification
techniques / Kenneth D. Bailey.
        p. cm. — (Quantitative applications in the social sciences ; 07-102)
    Includes bibliographical references.
    ISBN 0-8039-5259-7 (pb)
        1. Social sciences—Classification. 2. Social sciences—
Methodology.   I. Title.   II. Series: Sage university papers
series. Quantitative applications in the social sciences; no. 07-102.
    H61.2.B34   1994
    300′.12—dc20
                                                                94-7960

03 04 10 9 8 7 6 5 4

Sage Production Editor: Astrid Virding

When citing a university paper, please use the proper form. Remember to cite the current Sage University Paper series title and include the paper number. One of the following formats can be adapted (depending on the style manual used):

(1) BAILEY, KENNETH D. (1994) *Typologies and Taxonomies: An Introduction to Classification Techniques.* Sage University Paper series on Quantitative Applications in the Social Sciences, 07-102. Thousand Oaks, CA: Sage.

OR

(2) Bailey, K. D. (1994). *Typologies and taxonomies: An introduction to classification techniques* (Sage University Paper series on Quantitative Applications in the Social Sciences, series no. 07-102). Thousand Oaks, CA: Sage.

CONTENTS

SERIES EDITOR'S INTRODUCTION

Classification is basic to the social sciences but seldom receives methodological exposition, perhaps because it is so ingrained in research practice. Professor Bailey's volume thus affords a rare opportunity for systematic reflection on this vital set of techniques. Classification involves the ordering of cases in terms of their similarity and can be broken down into two essential approaches: typology and taxonomy. The former is primarily conceptual, the latter empirical.

Construction of a typology requires conceptualization along at least two dimensions. To illustrate, consider the following hypothetical example. Dr. Alice Auburn, political scientist, develops a typology of nations, in terms of a political system dimension—Democratic versus Authoritarian—and an economic system dimension—Market versus Controlled. She then has a four-cell table, with each cell labeled a "type" of nation; for example, those in the Authoritarian/Controlled cell called a Totalitarian type, those in the Authoritarian/Market cell called a Traditional type. Since this is the simplest of typologies, she has little trouble naming all the cells. If she decides to add dimensions (or categories within the current dimensions), however, she will quickly multiply the number of "types" and so may wish to resort to a "reduction" procedure, carefully described by Professor Bailey.

A taxonomy begins empirically, rather than conceptually, with the goal of classifying cases according to their measured similarity on observed variables. The principal technique here is cluster analysis. Suppose, to continue our hypothetical example, Dr. Auburn focuses on a sample of 16 Latin American nations (cases) measured on 100 variables taken from U.N. Statistical Yearbooks. She applies Ward's hierarchial clustering method (a widely used agglomerative, objective, average linkage procedure) and finds that the nations group themselves into two distinct clusters. Conceptually, what do these clusters represent? Perhaps the more democratic nations are in one group, the more authoritarian in another. However, as Professor Bailey sagely points out, the cluster solution does not speak to the conceptual meaning of the clusters, but instead confines itself to demonstration of their empirical presence.

There are so many varieties of cluster analysis that the novice, not to mention the expert, risks bewilderment. Fortunately, Professor Bailey patiently describes each, along with advantages and disadvantages. In a masterful example of classification and summation, he offers a "Typology of Clustering Methods" (see Table 3.4), reducing most of them to two dimensions (form of linkage, type of similarity level) in six cells. Besides this valuable synthesis, he relates cluster analysis to factor analysis, multidimensional scaling, multiple discriminant analysis, and systems analysis. For the different classification procedures, conceptual or empirical, Professor Bailey provides comparative, thorough coverage, always in a writing style clear to student and faculty alike. All social science researchers will learn from this unique volume.

—*Michael S. Lewis-Beck*
—Series Editor

TYPOLOGIES AND TAXONOMIES
An Introduction to Classification Techniques

KENNETH D. BAILEY
University of California, Los Angeles

1. TYPOLOGIES AND TAXONOMIES IN SOCIAL SCIENCE

This monograph is about methods of classification. Classification is a very central process in all facets of our lives. It is so ubiquitous that not only do we generally fail to analyze it, we often even fail to recognize its very existence. Classification is arguably one of the most central and generic of all our conceptual exercises. It is the foundation not only for conceptualization, language, and speech, but also for mathematics, statistics, and data analysis in general. Without classification, there could be no advanced conceptualization, reasoning, language, data analysis or, for that matter, social science research. Yet, as central as this process is, it is often poorly understood. It is almost the methodological equivalent of electricity—we use it every day, yet often consider it to be rather mysterious. It is one of those things that we all use without knowing very much about how it works.

In its simplest form, classification is merely defined as the ordering of entities into groups or classes on the basis of their similarity. Statistically speaking, we generally seek to minimize within-group variance, while maximizing between-group variance. This means that we arrange a set of entities into groups, so that each group is as different as possible from all other groups, but each group is internally as homogeneous as possible. By maximizing both within-group homogeneity and between-group heterogeneity, we make groups that are as distinct (nonoverlapping) as possible, with all members within a group being as alike as possible. These are general goals that specific classification techniques may alter somewhat.

1

As just defined, classification is both a process and an end result. We may thus speak both of the process of classification and of a classification so formed.

Almost everything is classified to some degree in everyday life, from chewing gum (bubble and nonbubble), to people (men and women), to animals, to vegetables, to minerals. Grouping objects by similarity, however, is not quite as simple as it sounds. Imagine that we throw a mixture of 30 knives, forks, and spoons into a pile on a table and ask three people to group them by "similarity." Imagine our surprise when three different classifications result. One person classifies into two groups of utensils, the long and the short. Another classifies into three classes—plastic, wooden, and silver. The third person classifies into three groups—knives, forks, and spoons. Whose classification is "best"?

To belabor the example, suppose we secure survey data from a sample of 100 persons. We ask three people to classify this sample by "physical characteristics." One person produces the expected grouping into women and men. The second groups by height, producing one class of persons 5 feet 8 inches tall or more (mostly men but some women), and another class of persons under 5 feet 8 inches tall (mostly women, but some men). The third person produces a similar group based on weight, with the class of persons over 160 pounds containing both men and women (but mostly men), while the class under 160 pounds also contains both men and women (but mostly women). Again, which classification is the "best"?

The lesson here should be obvious—a classification is no better than the dimensions or variables on which it is based. If you follow the rules of classification perfectly but classify on trivial dimensions, you will produce a trivial classification. As a case in point, a classification that they have four legs or two legs may produce a four-legged group consisting of a giraffe, a dining-room table, and a dancing couple. Is this what we really want?

One basic secret to successful classification, then, is the ability to ascertain the key or fundamental characteristics on which the classification is to be based. A person who classifies mixtures of lead and gold on the basis of weight alone will probably be sadder but wiser. It is crucial that the fundamental or defining characteristics of the phenomenon be identified. Unfortunately, there is no specific formula for identifying key characteristics, whether the task is theory construction, classification, or statistical analysis. In all of these diverse cases, prior knowledge and theoretical guidance are required in order to make the right decisions.

Assuming that the fundamental dividing characteristics can be identified, the classification process often becomes very simplistic. It does not take a genius to separate white beans from black beans. Often the classification process merely consists of such simple divisions into groups. In such cases it can be accomplished by almost anyone, simply by observing the similar objects and grouping them together. The problem is that empirical classification problems are seldom so simple. The world is very complex. The difficulty of grouping by similarity grows exponentially with the number of objects to be classified and the number of dimensions on which they are being grouped. Thus while classifying 10 beans by color is simplicity itself, classifying 5 billion people on the basis of two thousand variables is another matter entirely. Even such a complex problem is relatively straightforward. We could conceivably simply match each of the 5 billion persons, two at a time, on all two thousand variables. This is not intellectually taxing, but is tremendously time consuming and likely overwhelms even the largest computer. Thus, for very large samples and many variables, some shorthand methods such as clustering algorithms or formulas need to be devised.

Another problem with classification procedures is that, like theory and data analysis, they can encompass at least three levels of analysis. These are the conceptual (where only concepts are classified), the empirical (where only empirical entities are classified), and the combined conceptual/empirical level (called the operational or indicator level by Bailey, 1990), where both are combined. In the latter, a conceptual classification is first devised, and then empirical examples of some or all of the cells are subsequently identified.

Basic Concepts

The generic classification process, as defined above, is quite simple. The only basic rule is that the classes formed must be both *exhaustive* and *mutually exclusive*. This means that if N persons are to be classified, there must be an appropriate class for each (exhaustivity), but only one correct class for each, with no case being a member of two classes (mutual exclusivity). Thus, there must be one class (but only one) for each of the N persons.

Although the basic definition of classification is simple, the complexity of the cases to which it is addressed makes it complicated, as noted above. This leads to a plethora of definitions, many of them quite arcane. It is crucial that the student of classification not get so confused by all of the terms that he or she is unable to see the forest for the trees. The following terms are the minimum set of basic concepts.

Classification. Already defined, classification is the general process of grouping entities by similarity. Classification can either be *unidimensional,* being based solely on a single dimension or characteristic, or *multidimensional,* being based on a number of dimensions. When multidimensional, the dimensions are generally thought to be correlated or related, as in the four rational dimensions (compensatory rewards, specialization, performance emphasis, and segmental participation) discussed in Chapter 2. Unrelated dimensions generally would not be combined in a classification, but could be. Dimensions are generally categorical data, such as nominal or ordinal variables. Interval and ratio variables can be used as well, however, if the researcher first categorizes them. Further, quantified cluster methods can use variables of all levels—nominal, ordinal, interval, or ratio—as discussed in Chapter 3.

Typology. Typology is another term for a classification. Two characteristics distinguish typologies from generic classifications. A typology is generally *multidimensional* and *conceptual.* Typologies generally are characterized by labels or names in their cells. As a hypothetical example, let us use two dimensions to construct a classification. These dimensions are intelligence (dichotomized as intelligent/unintelligent) and motivation (dichotomized as motivated/unmotivated). Combining these two dimensions creates a fourfold typology, as shown in Table 1.1. These four categories can be defined as *cells* in the table. In this case, they are *types,* or *type concepts.* A motivated and intelligent person can be labeled as successful; an intelligent but unmotivated person is likely to be an underachiever; while a motivated but unintelligent person is an overachiever; and one who lacks both intelligence and motivation is likely doomed to failure.

A problem is that if the number of dimensions is large, and the number of categories in each dimension is also large, the typology may contain a great many cells or types. For example, even if all dimensions are dichotomies, the formula for determining the number of cells is 2^M, where M is the number of dimensions. Thus, for five dichotomous dimensions the typology will contain only 2^5 or 32 cells, but for 12 dichotomous dimensions the number of cells is 2^{12} or 4,096. If the dimensions are polytomous rather than dichotomous, as is often the case, the number of cells expands much more rapidly. Because the number of types can be so large, re-

TABLE 1.1
A Hypothetical Fourfold Typology

	Motivated	Unmotivated
Intelligent	Success 1	Underachiever 2
Unintelligent	Overachiever 3	Failure 4

searchers have often found it helpful to use partial or shorthand typologies. These can be formed either by constructing only a portion of the full typology or by first constructing the full typology and then selecting only certain types for use in the analysis (or by merging some types together).

For example, if we wish to construct a typology from seven dichotomous variables, we may find it difficult to work with all of the 128 resulting types. It may be that only a few chief types are found to be really important to our work, so that we may focus on these and neglect the remainder. Alternatively, it may turn out that a number of types (perhaps an unknown number) are needed, but not the entire typology. In such cases it is common to utilize a shorthand typology by first constructing only key *criteria types,* and then locating all other types in reference to these criteria.

For example, we could define as a criterion type, the type with the highest values on all dimensions. Then other types could be measured in terms of their deviation from this criterion. Often two polar types are used. *Polar types* are two extreme opposite types (such as the type scoring highest on all dimensions and the type scoring lowest on all dimensions). All remaining types would be intermediate to the polar types, and could be located in terms of their deviation from these two cells. This allows a researcher to leave the majority of cells latent and to construct only those cells that have representative types, as measured by their deviation from a criterion type or polar types.

Conceptual Classification. A typology is seen to be a conceptual classification. The cells of the typology represent type concepts rather than empirical cases.

Qualitative Classification. The typologies discussed so far can be identified as qualitative classifications, because they can generally be formed without quantification or statistical analysis, unlike the clustering methods to be discussed later. Further, the typologies discussed so far are entirely verbal and conceptual, lacking empirical cases. Even when empirical cases are identified for such typologies, this can often be accomplished without quantification.

Taxonomy. Like *classification,* the term *taxonomy* can refer to both the process and the end result. As a process, we can adopt Simpson's (1961) definition of taxonomy as "the theoretical study of classification, including its bases, principles, procedures and rules" (p. 11). Sneath and Sokal (1973, p. 3) would enlarge this definition to include the theoretical study of identification (discussed later in this chapter) as well.

As an end result, a taxonomy is similar to a typology, and in fact many people use the two terms interchangeably. Here we will reserve the term *taxonomy* for a classification of empirical entities. The basic difference, then, is that a typology is conceptual while a taxonomy is empirical. Exceptions to this generally involve the subsequent identification of empirical cases for conceptual typologies, but not the conceptualization of taxonomies. One cell of a taxonomy is a *taxon.* Multiple cells are *taxa.* The term *taxonomy* is more generally used in the biological sciences, while *typology* is used in the social sciences. Taxonomies are often (but not always) hierarchical (as in family, genus, species) and evolutionary.

Numerical Taxonomy. A numerical taxonomy is a quantitative, usually computerized method for constructing taxonomies. The term originated in biology (see Sokal & Sneath, 1963).

Operational Taxonomic Unit. Also a biological term, *operational taxonomic unit* (OTU) refers to the basic unit used in the numerical analysis. Often the OTU is an individual organism, but it could be a group or some other unit (see Sneath & Sokal, 1973, pp. 68-75).

Cluster Analysis. A cluster analysis is also a quantitative method of classification. This term originated in psychology, where the related term of *pattern analysis* is also used (see Bailey, 1974). Although cluster techniques predate computerization with some being developed in the 1930s or earlier (Bailey, 1974), most are now computerized. The terms *numerical taxonomy* and *cluster analysis* are thus not mutually exclusive, but are in fact virtually synonymous. There could be some psychologists or others who would not wish to designate their clustering methods as numerical taxonomy, but most techniques of numerical taxonomy can be identified as clustering algorithms.

Quantitative Classification. Methods of numerical taxonomy and cluster analysis are quantitative methods. This is in contrast to typological methods, which we have previously identified as qualitative.

Empirical Classification. Taxonomic methods are empirical methods. They generally begin with a data set of empirical objects (such as individuals) measured on a number of variables. Various techniques, usually quantitative, are then used to group the cases by overall similarity on the variables.

Monothetic Classes. Monothetic classes are classes containing cases that are all identical on all variables or dimensions being measured. Typologies generally contain only monothetic classes (i.e., a type is a monothetic class). Referring back to the typology previously presented in Table 1.1, all persons in Type 1 would be both intelligent and motivated (no exceptions), while all persons in Type 4 would be unintelligent and unmotivated (no exceptions). Conceptual types are generally defined monothetically.

Polythetic Classes. In contrast to monothetic classes, polythetic classes do not contain cases that are identical on all variables, but rather group cases by overall greatest similarity. For example, Case 1 and Case 2 might be similar on variables 1 and 2, while Case 1 and Case 3 are similar on variables 1 and 3. Thus Cases 1, 2, and 3 are not identical on variables 1, 2, and 3, but share an overall similarity greater than the similarity with cases in other classes. That is, they are more similar to the cases in their class than to the cases in other classes. As defined by Beckner (1959, p. 22) a monothetic class requires all cases to have a set of properties that are both necessary and sufficient. In contrast, a polythetic class is defined differently. We can define a polythetic class in terms of a set G of properties $f_1, f_2, \ldots, f_n$ such that:

1. Each one possesses a large (but unspecified) number of the properties in G
2. Each f in G is possessed by large numbers of these individuals

3. No f in G is possessed by every individual in the aggregate. (Beckner, 1959, p. 22)

A class is called polythetic if just the first two conditions are fulfilled, and fully polythetic if all three are fulfilled. That is, a class is fully polythetic if the objects in it do not share even a single characteristic in common.

Systematics. Systematics is defined by Simpson (1961, p. 7) as "the scientific study of the kinds and diversity of organisms and of any and all relationships among them."

Natural Classification. The term *natural classification* has been used in a number of ways, particularly in biological classification (see Sneath & Sokal, 1973). Here we will use it to refer to a system that occurs naturally in the empirical world, as contrasted with an artificial system, which has no natural occurrence prior to its construction by the researcher. See Chapter 3 for further discussion of this topic.

Synchronic Classification. Most classification in social science is synchronic or cross-sectional, meaning that it occurs at a single point in time. Such synchronic or nonevolutionary relationships are sometimes termed *phenetic relationships* in biology (see Sokal & Sneath, 1963).

Diachronic Classification. Although more difficult, it is also possible to utilize diachronic classification based, for example, on measures of change or on measures of evolutionary resemblance. Before numerical taxonomy, much classification in biology was diachronic, based on evolution. Relationships showing the course of evolution are termed *phyletic.* Phyletic similarity consists of patristic and of cladistic relationships. In patristic relationships, two organisms share many characteristics derived from a common ancestor. In cladistic relationships, the common ancestry is recent. Patristic relationships are, strictly speaking, synchronic and are also a part of phenetic relationships, while cladistic relationships are strictly diachronic. For further discussion see Sneath and Sokal (1973, pp. 27-60).

Identification of Cases. Notice that the typology of success and failure presented in Table 1.1 was constructed without knowing how many (or if any) empirical cases could be found for a given cell. I call the process of finding empirical cases for a cell in a typology or taxonomy *identification.*

As we shall see, many taxonomies, especially those produced by numerical-taxonomic methods, actually identify cases as part of the process of taxonomy construction. That is, they first measure various aspects of empirical cases, and then group these cases by overall similarity, thus forming taxa. Thus the processes of taxonomy construction and identification are virtually synonymous.

In the case of verbal typologies, the types are first constructed, and then empirical cases are sought. Thus, the processes of typology construction and identification of cases are here quite separate. Even for empirically constructed taxonomies, however, new cases can be identified through such methods as multiple discriminant analysis. That is, one might combine 100 cases into eight taxa, then undertake a new survey of an additional 10 cases, each of which can subsequently be identified as belonging to one of the eight taxa. Thus, the process of identification can be accomplished for both conceptual and empirical classifications.

Nomenclature. Another term pertaining to the general classification process is *nomenclature*. Nomenclature refers to the names for parts of a given entity. For example, the nomenclature of a rifle consists of the names for its various parts, such as the trigger, barrel, firing pin, and so forth.

Subtypes or Subtaxa or Subclasses. Often after constructing types, taxa, or other classes, we can subdivide these still further. Such "types of types" are called subtypes. For example, we might classify United States coins into dollars, half dollars, quarters, dimes, nickels, and cents. Then the subclass of cents would be flying-eagle cents, Indian head cents, Lincoln cents, and so forth. The subclass of Lincoln cents could further be divided into sub-subclasses by date, and into sub-sub-subclasses by mint marks within each date. It may be possible to divide a class into a number of different levels or subclasses.

Property Space. All classifications are composed of at least one dimension or variable, and most of two or more. When these dimensions are combined, they are said to form a property space (Barton, 1955). If the variables so combined are discrete, then the resulting property space is like the one in Table 2.1 in Chapter 2. Table 2.1 is a four-dimensional space, composed of the combination of four variables: compensatory rewards, specialization, performance emphasis, and segmental participation. If the variables forming the dimensions are continuous, then the result is the familiar coordinate space, as shown in Figure 3.1 in Chapter 3.

The definitions just presented are not exhaustive. They do, however, provide the basic terminology to begin our discussion. Some of the terms defined here will be explicated in more detail later in this volume, and additional terms will be defined and discussed as needed.

The History of Classification in Social Science

Social science classification techniques have developed through a number of distinct stages. It is perhaps easiest to understand how current techniques have developed by briefly examining the history of the field. The later chapters will generally follow the chronology sketched here. For further discussion of classification history, see also Sokal and Sneath (1963), McKinney (1966), Tiryakian (1968), and Bailey (1974, 1992).

While numerous classification schemes have been widely developed throughout the history of social science by many authors, and applied in a wide variety of areas, the best known and most rigorously elaborated conceptual or qualitative typological schemes were derived by the German sociologists Max Weber (1947, 1949), and later Howard Becker (1940, 1950, 1951). Weber is well known for his analysis of the *ideal type,* while Becker and his student John McKinney (see McKinney, 1966) later popularized the related notion of the *constructed type.* Although both the ideal type and the constructed type are criterion types as defined previously, they represent distinctly different strategies. The ideal type is an extreme or heightened representation of all dimensions in the typology, and thus is the equivalent of the high end of a yardstick or the top of a range of values. The constructed type, in contrast, is a description of the most commonly found characteristics, and is thus analogous to a measure of central tendency such as a mean, rather than to the end point of a continuum, as is the ideal type.

Both of these forms represent rather ingenious strategies for dealing with large masses of data in a time long before the advent of computers. Although some of the goals of such types are more efficiently met through modern computerized methods of numerical taxonomy, these types still retain considerable epistemological value and have a distinct role in the modern classification armory, particularly if their relationship to quantitative methods is clearly understood. These early types are the topic of Chapter 2.

The next phase in the development of classification procedures was the advent of precomputerized quantitative techniques such as cluster analysis. While interest in qualitative typological methods began in earnest in the 19th century (and even earlier), and has lasted until the present, the early clustering methods were invented largely in the period from the 1930s to the 1960s without the benefit of computerization. The computer was in existence in the latter part of the period, yet some analysts such as McQuitty (1957) continued to devise algorithms that could be utilized without computers. While precomputer factor analysis was a long and tedious process, which sometimes lasted for weeks (see Fruchter, 1954), most cluster analyses of the time could be performed quite quickly. The bulk of these were agglomerative methods that proceeded by first finding a nucleus for the cluster, and then following some formula for adding subsequent additional members to the cluster.

Later methods devised from the late 1950s and early 1960s through the present, are almost exclusively computerized methods. They tend to be either more complex agglomerative methods or divisive methods. Divisive methods in particular were greatly advanced through computerization, as the high level of computation involved makes the use of divisive methods quite limited without computerization. These various clustering procedures are defined and discussed in Chapter 3. These include both early and more recent techniques, including both agglomerative and divisive methods. Chapter 4 shows the relationships among various techniques, including the relationship of monothetic, qualitative typologies to quantitative, polythetic taxonomies. Clustering methods are also compared with each other and with related statistical techniques such as factor analysis, multiple discriminant analysis, multidimensional scaling, and systems analysis. Chapter 5, the final chapter, evaluates the current state of classification in social science.

It may be helpful to conclude this chapter with a discussion of both the goals of the classification process and the advantages of classification, followed by a discussion of the limitations of classification, and some criticisms of its use in social science.

Advantages and Disadvantages of Classification

Advantages

There are a number of distinct advantages that make classification not only ubiquitous, but in fact necessary. It is necessary not only in social science research, but, as indicated previously, in virtually all of everyday life. Some of the primary advantages of classification are listed here.

1. Description. Classification is the premier descriptive tool. A good classification allows the researcher to provide an exhaustive and perhaps even definitive array of types or taxa. Not only are all types listed, but they are listed in a side-by-side format that allows the researcher to ascertain quickly how a particular type scores on a particular dimension and which types are contiguous to a particular type. For example, the typology presented previously in Table 1.1 shows that the type of "successful" person is described or defined as a person who is high on both intelligence and motivation.

2. Reduction of Complexity. Another chief goal of classification is to reduce complexity or achieve parsimony. The population of the United States exceeds 250 million people. There are scores if not hundreds of salient variables that we might measure for each of these persons. This would provide a matrix of truly staggering proportions. If we were not able to classify persons, objects, and concepts into a smaller number of similar classes, it is doubtful that we could manage to describe such a population and its myriad characteristics at all. Although we cannot focus upon all persons and all of their characteristics at once, by classifying persons according to salient underlying dimensions such as race, social class, age, sex, political party, religion, and so forth, we can simplify our complex reality sufficiently to allow us to analyze it. Often typologies and taxonomies prove to be amazingly successful, allowing us to condense huge masses of data about populations or concepts into a small number of salient types or taxa.

For example, if we have data on 40 variables for each of 400 cities, we may find it extremely difficult to convey to our audience the entire meaning and significance of these 16,000 pieces of data. If, however, we can classify all 400 cities as belonging to one of only three taxa—manufacturing centers, service centers, or recreational centers—our task of communicating is greatly simplified.

3. Identification of Similarities. Classification procedures allow us to recognize similarities among cases, and group similar cases together for analysis, without having to concentrate on very different cases that may not be of immediate interest. The identification of similarities is the key to medical diagnosis, for example. If we can identify cases as being similar, we can find the persons that suffer from identical symptoms. This done, we are in a position to identify the underlying illness. If we are unable to determine such similarities, then the symptoms and the causes go undetected, and the persons suffering from the diseases cannot be identified. For example, the crucial first step in studying the Acquired Immune Deficiency Syndrome (AIDS) was to identify its symptoms, so that similar cases having similar symptoms can be classified and grouped together.

4. Identification of Differences. Similarly, classification procedures allow us to differentiate between different cases, so that dissimilar cases can be separated for analysis, rather than remaining mixed together. This is the other side of the coin. Often unidimensional classification will not suffice in medical diagnosis, for example. In fact, it may be necessary to check patients on six or seven characteristics before their actual disease can be differentiated from another disease. To use the language introduced earlier, two diseases may match on (be monothetic on) six symptoms, differing only on the seventh. It is only by studying two patients on all seven dimensions simultaneously that we can differentiate the two diseases, and discern that one patient has disease A while the other has disease B.

5. Presenting an Exhaustive List of Dimensions. A good typology not only shows an exhaustive set of types, it also shows the exhaustive set of dimensions on which the types are based. It is thus very comprehensive. Further, it shows the relationships between the types and dimensions, in the sense that each type is located on all dimensions

6. Comparison of Types. A good typology also allows the researcher quickly and easily to compare types. The researcher can select types in different areas of the typology (e.g., in the corners and in the center), and compare them. This gives a quick appraisal of the similarities and variation in the typology and of the general qualities inherent in the typology.

7. The Inventory and Management of Types. The full typology is the best inventory tool a researcher has. It allows him or her quickly to locate any needed type, and to know at all times what types are available for analysis.

8. The Study of Relationships. Although typologies are often seen as purely descriptive (rather than explanatory) tools, they often provide for the study of relationships and even the specification of hypotheses concerning these relationships. This is done by a combination of typology construction and identification of empirical cases for the cells of the typology. A typology where cases are randomly distributed among all cells will not exhibit relationships among dimensions. In contrast, when all empirical cases fall into a few cells within a large typology, with the other cells containing none or only a few cases, this is generally an indication of relationships among the dimensions or variables used to form the typology.

9. Types as Criteria for Measurement. As mentioned above, often one or a few types provide convenient tools for measurement. One type is selected as a criterion, and others are located in the property space by measuring how they relate to the criterion.

10. Versatility. A good classification is very versatile. This is perhaps the only format available to the social scientist for displaying either concepts or, alternatively, concrete empirical cases, or even a conjoint conceptual/empirical classification. For example, the results of a regression analysis show relationships among variables, but provide no information about the sample of persons from which the data were gathered. Conversely, an ethnographic study may provide a description of the persons who were observed, but provides little systematic quantitative knowledge about important theoretical concepts or variables. In contrast, a good classification can not only represent the persons studied, but also locate them within a property space formed by combining the variables utilized in the analysis.

Disadvantages

Because we have discussed how classifications are ubiquitous and necessary to all of social research, we might assume that they are universally championed by social researchers. Although the importance of classification is widely recognized in biology and psychiatry, for example, social scientists have been more critical of classification and have not always understood it very well. Among their criticisms are the following.

1. Classification Is Descriptive, Pre-Explanatory, or Nonexplanatory.
As noted previously, classification is the premier descriptive tool. This is
clearly an advantage and makes it fundamental in social science. The
research goals of explanation and prediction have been so widely touted
in social science, however, that some researchers tend to stereotype
classification as inadequate in these terms. They see it as "merely descriptive" or "pre-theoretical," as if this somehow makes it insufficient rather
than the prerequisite for theorizing that it is. Rather than dismissing
classification as failing to meet the goal of explanation, social scientists
should understand how necessary it is as a foundation for explanation.
Theory cannot explain much if it is based on an inadequate system of
classification.

2. Reification. Classical verbal typologies (including the ideal and
constructed types) share with all verbal theories the perils of reification.
That is, they are vulnerable to the possibility that theoretical constructs
that do not exist empirically will be "reified" and treated as "real"
empirical entities. It is true that there has sometimes been confusion about
whether a type was a construct or an empirical entity. However, this
problem can generally be avoided with a little care in the specification of
types.

3. Static Classification. Another common criticism is that classification may be static rather than dynamic. Unfortunately many research
approaches in social science, including most popular statistical techniques, are synchronic (static) rather than diachronic (dynamic). Thus,
although some classifications may seem inherently static, so does regression analysis. While this criticism is valid in some cases, it should not be
exaggerated. In the case of conceptual typologies, static typologies may
suffice. In the use of empirical taxonomies, the problems with static
analysis are probably no greater in numerical taxonomy than in statistics
in general, and may be accepted as a limitation of the statistical method.
In fact, some of the problems stem not from the classification procedures
per se, but from the statistical measures that they incorporate.

Further, time can often be introduced into the classification process just
as it can be in other areas of analysis, such as through the use of time-series
data or change coefficients. A particular problem in biological numerical
taxonomy is that some taxonomists are not satisfied with methods that are
merely dynamic or diachronic, but insist further that taxonomies have an

evolutionary basis. The inclusion of evolution is sometimes a problem for numerical taxonomy. For further discussion see Sneath and Sokal (1973, pp. 27-60).

4. Identification of Cases and Variables. Another alleged problem is the difficulty of selecting dimensions and finding cases for classifications. Though this may be true, this again is a problem for all of social research and is not unique to the classification process. It is true that the resulting classification is directly shaped by the selection of variables, but the same is true of regression analysis, for example. As noted previously, there is no magic formula for selecting the correct variables, but care and foresight generally result in successful typologies.

5. Unmanageability. Another criticism of classification is that while small ones may be simplistic and of limited value, very large ones may be unmanageable and too complex to use efficiently. This problem may be alleviated with computerized cluster analysis methods, but even then it can be a problem, and computer capacity can be exceeded. It is just such problems of unmanageability that probably stimulated the use of short-hand typologies, and the use of criterion types, as discussed in Chapter 2. Further, as noted, one goal of classification is to reduce complexity and insure manageability. Thus, if a study seems unmanageable when properly classified, just think how much more unmanageable it would be without classification.

6. The Logic of Classes. Typologies have sometimes been criticized for depending upon the logic of classes, rather than utilizing continuous data, as do modern statistical techniques. To some degree this criticism is obsolete, as the methods of numerical taxonomy discussed in Chapter 3 definitely do not depend on the logic of classes. While they often utilize dichotomous (binary) data, they can use continuous data as well. Further, while the typological methods of Chapter 2 do often rely on the logic of classes, this in and of itself is not negative, especially if the relationship of such monothetic typologies to polythetic types is made clear, as is done in Chapter 4. For further discussion of the advantages and disadvantages of evaluation see Bailey (1989) and Kreps (1989).

So far we have presented basic definitions of classification and have briefly traced the history of the field. We have also examined some advantages and disadvantages of classification. It is now time to begin Chapter 2, where we examine verbal typologies in more detail.

2. CLASSICAL TYPOLOGY CONSTRUCTION (PRECOMPUTER)

The Ideal Type

Certainly the most famous type concept in social science is Weber's (1949) notion of the *ideal type*. Discussion about the ideal type has centered upon such questions as whether the type is real, a model, an if-then statement, a theory, or something derived from theory (see Hempel, 1952; Martindale, 1959, 1960; Winch, 1947). The confusion stems from the fact that Weber actually had different subtypes or versions of the ideal type. Weber's basic definition is clear:

> An ideal type is formed by the one-sided *accentuation* of one or more points of view. . . . In its conceptual purity, this mental construct (Gedankenbild) cannot be found empirically anywhere in reality. It is a utopia. Historical research faces the task of determining in each individual case the extent to which the ideal-construct approximates to or diverges from reality, to what extent for example, the economic structure of a city is to be classified as a city economy. (Weber, 1949, p. 90. Italics in the original.)

Parsons (1949, p. 60) says that the ideal type can indeed be found empirically, but only in a few very special cases. Parsons (1949, pp. 603-604) adds that the ideal type is not a hypothesis, a description of reality, an average, or a formulation of the traits common to a class of things.

In reality, Weber specified three varieties of the ideal type. Capecchi (1966, p. 14) refers to Weber's three ideal types as: (1) the nonabstract historical ideal type; (2) the nonabstract generalizable ideal type; and (3) the abstract ideal type. These are also known respectively as the individualizing type, the generalizing type, and the model. In addition, Weber sometimes called the ideal type a "pure" type.

There are two features of the ideal type that are the heart of the method, but that are also confusing and have led to much misunderstanding and controversy. These are Weber's contentions that: (1) the ideal type is not found empirically; and (2) the ideal type is used to study the degree to which a concrete empirical case differs from the ideal. The second feature follows from the first. If ideal types do not exist empirically, we can use them to study empirical examples only by studying deviation. Martindale is startled by the suggestion that:

we compare actual individuals with the (admittedly imaginary) ideal typical individuals to see how they deviate from them. This is nothing but a form of intellectual acrobatics, for actual individuals ought to deviate from the ideal type just as much as one made them deviate in the first place. (Martindale, 1960, p. 382)

Martindale also disagrees with the idea that the ideal type is an "if . . . then" proposition.

We can quickly dispose of much of the confusion regarding the ideal type by noting that only one of Weber's three chief subtypes—the nonabstract generalizable ideal type—is of primary utility as a typological technique. The historical ideal type (individualizing concept) is of more use as a theoretical device for verbal theorists. The abstract ideal type or model is the one that Weber used as an "if . . . then" device. This type entails envisioning what would happen in an ideal situation, and comparing it with what actually happens. Weber (1947, pp. 83-84) provides the example of a panic on the stock exchange. We can model this by saying, "If action on the stock exchange were purely rational, then what would happen?" We can contrast this purely rational model with the real-world situation where irrationality plays a big part in the panic. By contrasting the real with the "if . . . then" model of the purely rational, we are able to assess the effects of the irrational component. Although a useful modeling tool, this usage is not directly applicable to typological analysis.

The third subtype, however, the nonabstract generalizing type, is extremely valuable as a typological tool. Its chief value is as an ingenious noncomputerized means of dealing with the unmanageability produced by a large, complex, and unwieldy classification—a problem discussed in Chapter 1. We might think at first glance that the advent of computerization has rendered Weber's method obsolete and unnecessary, as computers can handle large classifications. This is generally true for the empirical taxonomic techniques to be discussed in Chapter 3, but not for the qualitative, conceptual typologies discussed in this chapter. Without quantification, the computer can be of relatively little value in the construction of complex conceptual typologies that are our focus here. Thus, although Weber's method is old, it remains the premier qualitative strategy for providing a shorthand approach to huge typologies.

The key to understanding Weber is the understanding of what he meant by "accentuation," and the statement that the type cannot, "in its conceptual purity," be found anywhere in reality, but is a utopia. Misunderstanding has been widespread because researchers have misinterpreted Weber as saying that the ideal type is "imaginary" [in Martindale's (1960, p. 382) words], or hypothetical. If this were true, the whole procedure would be silly. As Martindale says, the amount of deviation would then be constructed by the researcher, and the ideal type, not being fixed, could be moved around at will, thus increasing or decreasing the amount of deviation from the fixed empirical cases. All of the deviation would then in effect merely be purposefully constructed measurement error.

It seems clear to me that Weber was too serious and sensible a researcher to be advocating such a silly procedure. In fact, in my opinion, his procedure is not silly, but is pure genius. To understand it, however, we must understand what he meant by "accentuation" and "utopia." To begin with, the ideal type is not some hypothetical entity (such as a unicorn) without a fixed location in typological space. To the contrary, it is an empirical entity with a fixed position, and its position cannot be moved in order to vary the amount of deviation from other types or cases. What Weber was trying to describe was not a moveable, hypothetical type or a "fiction" or imaginary entity, but rather the ultimate criterion type. By asking ourselves what characteristics the perfect criterion would have, we can better understand Weber's reasoning. If I were designing the perfect criterion type, I would want a type that: (a) possessed all of the relevant features or dimensions of the type; (b) exhibited extreme clarity on all features. Thus, I would insist that no dimensions of the type be missing or unrepresented in my criterion example. Further, I would insist that none of the dimensions be blurred, dull, impure, illegible, ambiguous, or similarly difficult to discern. I would wish for the clearest and purest example of the type, with no dull or damaged features. In short, I would like to have a perfect specimen.

Now, I ask you rhetorically, how often is the perfect specimen found empirically? Or stated another way, is the absolutely perfect specimen ever found empirically in this less-than-perfect world? To follow up this point, if the perfect specimen were to be found empirically, would not the wear and tear of the "real" world quickly mar its perfection, rendering it less suitable as a criterion?

In my opinion, this larger-than-life quality is all that Weber was referring to in describing the ideal type. Rereading the quote above, it is clear that Weber never said that the ideal type was not found empirically (in some form), was hypothetical, or was imaginary. Rather, what he said, was that it could not be found empirically "in its conceptual purity." Saying that a pure or ideal or perfect state or condition of something does not exist empirically is not tantamount to saying that the entity itself does not exist empirically in some less pure condition. The entity represented by the ideal type does exist empirically, just not in the purest state.

Perhaps the clearest example of this can be made with a numismatic analogy. If you wished to classify specimens of a particular type of coin, such as the 20 dollar Saint Gaudens gold piece, what would you choose as the best criterion for classifying other pieces, a well-worn circulated example, or an uncirculated mint-state example? The answer is obvious. There would be consensus that the uncirculated coin would be the best criterion for judging other coins, as its features would all be present in the clearest form. The badly worn circulated specimen would be almost useless as a criterion, as its own features would be difficult to discern. Thus, its empirical status would actually be a detriment or liability, rather than an asset.

The purest criterion would probably be graded at about Mint State 70 (MS-70). An MS-70 coin will have all features perfectly represented. In reality the actual MS-70 is probably a utopia, or ideal type. It is doubtful that one would be found empirically. Empirical specimens can approach MS-70. Specimens grading MS-64 are common, and specimens of MS-65, MS-66, MS-67, or possibly even MS-68 might be found. A true MS-70 probably would not be found, although an artist's rendition could provide a picture of it. Is an MS-70 a flexible, moveable, hypothetical state? Not at all. It is a fixed, inflexible criterion point that cannot be duplicated. This is the purest, clearest picture of the coin. It is simply so accentuated or perfect on all features that a copy this pristine is unlikely to be found empirically (but this is not impossible). If such a pure state could be found empirically, it probably would not stay at MS-70 for very long, but would quickly become marred or worn, reducing it to a lesser state.

Coins in a condition that are easily found empirically (and reflect empirical wear) such as G-4 (Good), F-12 (Fine), and AU-50 (About Uncirculated) can all be graded (classified) in terms of how much they deviate from the ideal type of MS-70. Assuming that we graded these coins by observing five features in the obverse and five in the reverse, even dichotomization would yield a potential typology of 2^{10} or 1,024 possible grades of coins in the full typology. In reality, however, the wearing of the coin's features is not random, but is correlated and highly predictable (with some exceptions due to unusual circumstances).

Experienced classifiers know where wear will occur, and thus where to look on a coin (generally the high points will wear first). They know, for example, that wear on the features of the obverse is correlated with wear on the reverse. Thus, instead of occupying all 1,024 empirically possible cells, probably only about 70 cells or fewer of the typology will be used to house actual empirically found coin specimens. The other approximately 954 cells will be null and need not be even constructed, because they will not be used. That is, we can envision a continuum with a barely recognizable coin being graded zero, and the ideal type being graded MS-70 (instead of MS-1,024, as would be required if we had to use all possible cells of the typology), and roughly 69 intermediate grades being empirically possible.

Exactly the same sort of logic prevails in Weber's method. The ideal type is the clearest example of the type. It is the one formed by magnifying all features of the type, as with a magnifying glass. The researcher can begin with a typology such as the one just described with ten dimensions, forming potentially 1,024 cells. Obviously, a researcher cannot deal with so many concepts. Thus the typology is unmanageable, unless some way can be found to reduce the number of types from 1,024 to some more manageable number. This can be accomplished through various forms of typological reduction, to be discussed later in this chapter. In lieu of reduction techniques, Weber's ingenious strategy is to simply take the ideal type as a criterion point (or nucleus, if you will). It serves as the exemplar.

The straightforward strategy is, after the ideal type is described fully, to define all of the other 1,023 cells. After the types are specified in this full strategy, one can then turn to the identification of the empirical examples for all of the cells. One can see which of the 1,024 cells have empirical examples, and what the empirical frequency of each cell is. Because this is generally prohibitive, however, the ideal type strategy allows the researcher to eschew formulation of the other 1,023 conceptual types and to proceed directly to identification of empirical cases. This saves a tremendous amount of work. Once an empirical case is found, its position in the latent typology is specified by measuring its deviation from the ideal type. Only the types for which empirical cases exist then need to be specified in the typology, with all of the others remaining latent.

For example, pursuing our 10-dimensional example, let us code each dimension in a binary fashion, as either being present (+) or absent (−). The ideal type would then be the clearest or highest on all dimensions, or (+ + + + + + + + +). The exception to this is where some of the dimensions are inversely correlated with the others, in which case they could be negative (−) while the others were positive (+). For now, however, let us define the ideal type by all pluses. Suppose that in a study of empirical cases we found an example of (+ + − + − + + + +) and of

(+ + + + + − − − − −), and of (+ − + − + − + − + −). All other cells were null, and these 3 cells had frequencies respectively of 20, 10, and 20 out of a sample of 50 cases. In this instance we could conduct our entire analysis with only the ideal type and these 3 other cells, thus simplifying work greatly by allowing us to de-emphasize (but not entirely forget) the other potential 1,020 cells in the full typology. It is clear then that Weber's ideal-type strategy, rather than being an unworkable comparison with an imaginary case, is truly an ingenious strategy for conceptual typological analysis. It is really the only workable strategy for typologies so large and complex that they are otherwise unmanageable.

Thus, the ideal type need not be a utopia, and cannot be, to be most effective. It is best viewed as an extreme type, with the maximum values on all dimensions. These will generally be high values, but if some of the dimensions are negatively correlated then their extreme values will be low values. The feature of accentuation that Weber spoke of is best viewed as magnification, as when a researcher views an object through a magnifying glass. This makes it larger than life or accentuates it, but does not render it hypothetical or nonempirical in any way.

The Constructed Type

The constructed type is an outgrowth of the ideal type, as discussed primarily by Becker (1940) and McKinney (1954, 1966). It differs from the ideal type in that the constructed type is generally not an extreme or accentuated form of the type, but is rather a more common or central empirical form. As defined by McKinney, a constructed type is a:

> *purposive planned selection, abstraction, combination and (sometimes) accentuation of a set of criteria with empirical referents that serve as a basis for comparison of empirical cases.* (McKinney, 1966, p. 3. Italics in the original)

McKinney states further that:

> The comparison and measurement of empirical approximations reveal nothing but deviations from the construct. Nothing but "exceptions" to the constructed types exist. This is not only to be expected but is to be sought after for it is the basis of the typological method. (McKinney, 1954, p. 145)

The distinction between the ideal type and the constructed type can be clarified by comparing each of them with common statistical techniques.

In statistics we often compute an average such as a mean, and then measure deviation from it, for example, in terms of the variance or standard deviation. For a simple example, assume that we had six scores for a variable: 2, 2, 3, 3, 7, 7. Here the mean is 4 and the variance is 4.66. The range of scores is 5, from a low score of 2 to a high score of 7. The statistical strategy is to compute the mean (4) and see how much the six cases deviate from it. Using this strategy for the typological comparative method, we see that the respective deviations of the cases are −2, −2, −1, −1, +3, +3. We will call this practice of comparing deviation from a measure of central tendency such as the mean, Strategy A. We could alternatively compare all six cases not with the mean, but with the highest value (7), or the lowest value (2). Using 7 as a criterion, the respective cases deviate by −5, −5, −4, −4, 0, 0. We will call this Strategy B. We could also use the lowest score (2) as the criterion, yielding deviations of 0, 0, +1, +1, +5, +5. We will call this Strategy C.

As a rough approximation, the ideal type strategy is analogous to Strategy B (or possibly Strategy C). The constructed type utilizes a strategy which approximates Strategy A. Thus, the constructed type is analogous to a measure of central tendency (although McKinney, 1966, stresses that it is not merely an average). In contrast, the ideal type does not represent the center of the continuum, but rather one extreme end (usually the high end) of the range of values. Bear in mind that while our example here entails only one variable, ideal types are generally constructed of a number of variables or dimensions, perhaps 6 to 10, or even more.

Criterion types such as the ideal type and the constructed type serve a number of purposes as discussed previously. They are especially useful for reducing complexity, reducing the number of types needed, aiding comparisons, and defining multidimensional concepts. Polar types have the added advantage of delineating the range of types, by marking the opposite ends of the range. Examples of polar types include Tönnies's (1957) *Gemeinschaft* and *Gesellschaft* societies, Durkheim's (1893) mechanical and organic types of social solidarity, and Redfield's (1941) folk-urban types (often expressed as the folk-urban continuum). The best known example of the ideal type is Weber's (1958) type of bureaucracy.

An example of a constructed type is "The impotent German intellectual" (McKinney, 1966, pp. 208-209). This type comprises nine dimensions: (1) strong nationalism; (2) great respect for the German military; (3) fear of Russia so great that the Nazis are the lesser evil; (4) the view that the outside world and not Germany is responsible for the rise of

Hitler; (5) political inactivity; (6) limited opposition to Hitler; (7) rejections of collaboration with working-class opponents of the Nazis; (8) pride in intellectuality as an end in itself; and (9) self-pity.

Substruction

One problem encountered by readers is that criterion types such as the ideal and constructed types or polar types are often presented by the author without the full typology, and even without a description of their characteristics, as just presented for the impotent German intellectual. In many cases, specification of the full typology is desirable or even necessary. If no characteristics at all are presented, it is often very difficult to try to form a full typology. Assuming, however, that a clear description of the correlated dimensions underlying the criterion type can be ascertained, one is often able to replicate the full typology from them. This process of extending the dimensions of a single type in order to form the full typology of which it is a part is called *substruction* (Lazarsfeld, 1937). The opposite process is to begin with a full typology and eliminate some of its cells through various strategies. This is termed *reduction* (Lazarsfeld, 1937).

As an example of these two opposite procedures, consider Weber's ideal-type concept of bureaucracy. Both Stinchcombe (1959) and Udy (1959) found that this could be divided into two type concepts of (1) rational; and (2) bureaucratic administration. The four dimensions of the rational type (from Udy, 1958) are: (1) compensatory rewards (allocation of rewards from higher to lower positions); (2) specialization; (3) performance emphasis (rewards proportional to performance); and (4) segmental participation (participation based on contractual agreement). Udy (1958) presented these as "present versus absent" variables (see also Bailey, 1973).

By merely listing these we have completed the first step in substruction—the identification of all four needed dimensions underlying the rational type. Now to complete the process of substruction we simply combine these four dimensions, as in Table 2.1.

These four characteristics can be combined in tabular form in two dimensions in a number of ways, but always the same 16 cells will result (only with different positions in the table depending upon how the four dimensions are arranged—see Bailey, 1973). Notice that because the paper is limited to two dimensions, the only way that the four dimensional

TABLE 2.1

A Sixteen-Cell Typology Formed by Substruction From Weber's Four
Dimensions of Rational Administration as Discussed by Udy (1958).

	Variable 3: Performance Emphasis			
	Present (1)		*Absent (0)*	
Variable 1: *Compensatory Rewards*	*Variable 4:* *Segmental Participation*		*Variable 4:* *Segmental Participation*	
	Present (1)	*Absent (0)*	*Present (1)*	*Absent (0)*
Present (1)				
Variable 2: Specialization	(1,1,1,1)	(1,1,1,0)	(1,1,0,1)	(1,1,0,0)
Present (1)	1	2	3	4
Absent (0)	(1,0,1,1)	(1,0,1,0)	(1,0,0,1)	(1,0,0,0)
	5	6	7	8
Absent (0)				
Variable 2: Specialization	(0,1,1,1)	(0,1,1,0)	(0,1,0,1)	(0,1,0,0)
Present (1)	9	10	11	12
Absent (0)	(0,0,1,1)	(0,0,1,0)	(0,0,0,1)	(0,0,0,0)
	13	14	15	16

typology of Table 2.1 can be constructed is by "stacking" two dimensions
(any two) in the horizontal dimension, and two in the vertical dimension.

Table 2.1 can be used to represent the various type concepts discussed
so far. Notice that I have labeled each cell in terms of presence (coded 1)
or absence (coded 0) on each of the four respective variables (characteristics or dimensions). Thus, a type in cell 1 possesses all four dimensions (1, 1, 1, 1), while a type in cell 16 possesses none (0, 0, 0, 0). The
other 14 cells are intermediate. Just as every beehive has a queen, every
typology should have an ideal type. Where is the ideal type in Table 2.1?

Inspection shows that the only cell that truly fits the definition of an ideal type (extreme or accentuated on all features) is cell 1. Its polar opposite is cell 16.

Both of these extreme types facilitate comparison precisely because of their extremeness—they either possess all characteristics or lack all characteristics. As such, they are quite visible. Notice, however, that cells 4 and 13 are also polar types, but are not quite as extreme as cells 1 and 16. That is, although cells 1 and 16 vary by four characteristics, both cells 4 and 13 each possess two characteristics (but a different two). We can also say that cells 1 and 16 are unique, but notice that in reality each of the 16 cells is unique, in the sense that its respective set of attributes is not duplicated by any other cell. For example, cell 8 is the only one possessing (1, 0, 0, 0). Notice also that all 16 cells are monothetic.

But if cell 1 is the ideal type, and cell pairs of 1 and 16 and 4 and 13 are polar types, which cell would be a good constructed type? It is somewhat less clear just where a constructed type would be located in Table 2.1. We could search for empirical cases and see where they clustered. However, McKinney (1966) warns that the constructed type is not necessarily the most common type (the mode). Further, all 16 types can occur empirically. Because the constructed type is generally not an extreme type like the ideal type, let us rule out cells 1, 4, 13, and 16, and choose the constructed type from the other 12 remaining cells. I would probably choose one of the interior types (cells 6, 7, 10, or 11) as the constructed type. All of these minimize deviation. That is, because all of these possess two attributes each, no empirical case that we could find would deviate from any of these on more than two dimensions. Let us arbitrarily choose cell 10 as the constructed type. It possesses characteristics 2 and 3 (specialization and performance emphasis), but lacks characteristics 1 and 4 (compensatory rewards and segmental participation).

Reduction

Although the 16-cell typology of Table 2.1 is perhaps manageable, if we had a larger typology (e.g., 512, or 1,024 cells), we might need to reduce the number of cells to a more manageable level. Lazarsfeld (1937) identified three forms of reduction: functional reduction, arbitrary numerical reduction, and pragmatic reduction. As just noted, all 16 cells of Table 2.1 are monothetic. All cases assigned to a given cell will be identical on all four variables. For example, all empirical cases of cell 10 will be identical. They will possess specialization and performance emphasis (variables 2 and 3), but will lack compensatory rewards and segmental participation (variables 1 and 4).

Functional Reduction

Functional reduction maintains monotheticism, while pragmatic and arbitrary numerical reduction result in polythetic types. Functional reduction is the simplest form. It consists mainly of eliminating all null cells (those without empirical cases) in the typology. Assume that we could find empirical cases for cells 1, 2, 3, 4, 9, and 10 of Table 2.1, but none for cells 5, 6, 7, 8, 11, 12, 13, 14, 15, or 16. These latter 10 cells would be dropped from the working typology, leaving us with the partial (residual) typology of cells 1 through 4, 9, and 10. These remaining 6 cells would still be monothetic.

Pragmatic Reduction

Lazarsfeld's second form of reduction is pragmatic. This consists of collapsing contiguous cells together. For example, in Table 2.1 we could collapse around the ideal type of cell 1 (1, 1, 1, 1) by adding to it cells 2, 3, 5, and 9 (collapsing "around the corner"). Similarly we could collapse around the corner for its polar opposite of cell 16 (0, 0, 0, 0), adding to it cells 8, 12, 14, and 15. This would reduce the typology from 16 monothetic cells to 8 cells. Six of these would be monothetic. These are the noncollapsed original cells: 4, 6, 7, 10, 11, and 13. The other 2 cells would be the new polythetic reduced type 1 (originally cells 1, 2, 3, 5, and 9), and new polythetic reduced type 2 (originally cells 8, 12, 14, 15, and 16).

The first new polythetic type is the rational administrative type. It consists of all organizations that possess any three of the four characteristics: compensatory rewards, specialization, performance emphasis, or segmental participation. It is polythetic because, for example, both an organization that possessed the first three characteristics but lacked the fourth (cell 2) and an organization that possessed the last three characteristics but lacked the first (cell 9) would qualify as members of this type, even though they have only two characteristics in common (numbers 2 and 3).

The second new polythetic type (8, 12, 14, 15, 16) is the nonrational administrative type. All organizations in it contain a maximum of one rational characteristic. Like the rational type it is polythetic. A type is defined as *fully polythetic* if no characteristic is possessed by every case in the type. Thus, both types formed by pragmatic reduction can be seen to be fully polythetic. This is assured by the fact that a zero appears at least once for each of the four characteristics in each type, prohibiting them from being possessed by all cases.

Arbitrary Numerical Reduction

Lazarsfeld's third form of reduction is *arbitrary numerical*. Lazarsfeld (1937, p. 128) provided an example. He said that in studying housing conditions, we could weight plumbing without either central heat or a refrigerator equal to the other two without plumbing. Coding existence of a characteristic by 1 and absence by 0, and considering the variables in this order: plumbing, central heat, refrigerator, this means that $(1, 0, 0) = (0, 1, 1)$. Extending this to Table 2.1, we could say that $(1, 0, 0, 0) = (0, 1, 1, 1)$, or cell 8 = cell 9. Together these two types form a fully polythetic type, as a case need not possess all four characteristics (but as few as one) to be admitted to this type. Arbitrary numerical reduction is equivalent to folding over the typology thus rendering formerly distant types equal.

The uses of substruction and reduction should be clear. Substruction is used when the researcher is presented with too few types and wishes to construct either the full typology, or at least some of the other missing types in the typology. Reduction solves the opposite problem. It is needed when one has too many types, and manageability is thus a problem. Although one would not generally first use substruction to construct a full typology and then use reduction to return to the original types, nevertheless these procedures can be used together. One might first use substruction to construct the full typology, and then use reduction to construct different types than the original ones, or use pragmatic and/or arbitrary numerical reduction to construct polythetic types that can be compared with the original monothetic types.

Stinchcombe's Typological Analysis

We have said that one primary function of typologies is the reduction of complexity. Readers may see little evidence of this, however, when even a typology comprised of 10 dichotomous variables numbers 1,024 cells. Although this is certainly complex enough for the average person, we have just seen that this complexity can be greatly reduced by two strategies: (1) originally constructing only one or a few criterion types instead of the entire typology; or (2) creating the entire typology, but reducing its complexity through functional, pragmatic, or arbitrary-numerical reduction. A third strategy has been hinted at previously and was discussed explicitly by Stinchcombe (1968). He says that while typologies have different functions, one of these is most fundamental. In this case:

> A typology is a statement that a large number of variables have only a small number of combinations of values which actually occur, with all other combinations being rare or nonexistent. This results in a radical improvement in scientific theory. (Stinchcombe, 1968, p. 47)

Two things should be noted about this concentration of cases into only a few cells of the typology: (1) it indicates that the variables used to form the typology are intercorrelated; and (2) it is a sufficient (but not necessary) condition for functional reduction. As for the first case, reconsider Table 2.1. If the four variables in Table 2.1 are all uncorrelated, the distribution of empirical cases into the 16 cells will be random. The more correlation that exists among the four variables, the more grouping into a few cells we can expect. If all four variables are found to be very highly intercorrelated, all cases might clump along the main diagonal, perhaps into only two cells, the polar cells of 1 and 16. That is, when compensatory reward, specialization, performance emphasis, and segmental participation are all highly (ideally, perfectly) correlated, then when an organization possesses one, it will possess all four, and will be placed in cell 1. Conversely, if an organization lacks one of these variables, it will lack all four, and will be placed in cell 16. Thus a very high degree of positive intercorrelation could even place all cases in cells 1 and 16, leaving the other 14 cells vacant or null. This is for positive correlation. For negative correlation, cases would fall along the other diagonal, chiefly in cells 4 and 13.

When the variables comprising the typology are highly correlated so that all cases fall into a few cells, functional reduction is accomplished simply by removing the null cells from the typology. Although this is sufficient for functional reduction, it is not necessary. Functional reduction can be accomplished with a lower degree of correlation and with a more random distribution of empirical cases into cells, as long as at least one cell is null so that it can be removed from the typology. It is clear, however, that if the variables are not highly correlated, functional reduction may result in the reduction of only a few cells. If the variables are highly intercorrelated, functional reduction is maximized and may result in the reduction of the majority of cells in the typology. In the example just discussed, perfect correlation could result in the elimination of 14 cells out of 16, leaving only the polar types of cells 1 and 16.

We said in our definition of classification in Chapter 1 that the dimensions of a typology are generally thought to be interrelated, but need not always be. We just noted here that if the dimensions are indeed intercorrelated, this may result in empirical specimens being grouped into a few cells in the classification. This could occur if the dimensions were all related in a linear or additive fashion. Sometimes, however, dimensions are related in a nonlinear fashion, such as in a multiplicative relationship, which may indicate the existence of statistical interaction. When statistical interaction exists, the effect of one variable on a second variable is different, depending upon the value of a third variable.

Stinchcombe (1968, p. 46) says that such typologies for examining interaction effects are among the most common in sociology. As an example, return to Table 1.1. This can be seen to be a typology, with types in the cells, for analyzing interaction effects. Table 1.1 shows that the effect of intelligence on success depends on motivation. Thus, just being intelligent does not ensure success, but rather the effect of intelligence on success is different for different values of motivation. Stinchcombe (1968, p. 47) concludes that while such typologies for studying interaction are common, they are not as fundamental as those discussed above, in which a large number of variables have only a small number of combinations of values that actually occur.

Bailey's Three-Level Model

It is common in discussion of classification procedures to differentiate between the conceptual and empirical levels. This dichotomy may be labeled in various ways, including heuristic-empirical (Winch, 1947). In reality, work that I have published elsewhere (Bailey, 1984, 1986) shows conclusively that we routinely deal with three basic levels of reality in social research, instead of only two as it is commonly assumed.

I have labeled these three levels of reality the conceptual (X), the empirical (X'), and the operational or indicator levels (X"). These three levels are illustrated in Figure 2.1. The conceptual level is represented by a typology of purely conceptual types. These could even be hypothetical or imaginary constructs, with no empirical counterparts. Even if the constructs are not hypothetical, no empirical cases are identified for the

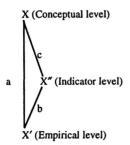

Figure 2.1. The Three-Level Measurement Model
SOURCE: Reprinted from K. D. Bailey (1984) "A Three-Level Measurement Model," *Quality and Quantity* 18: 235. Used by permission of Elsevier Science Publishers.

respective types. Such a conceptual typology is generally deductively derived. It may have theoretical significance, but no direct empirical counterpart. Conversely, it could be the case that these types would all have great empirical value. But this can only be determined through the measurement process, by identifying empirical cases for each type, and measuring the correspondence between the conceptual type (X) and its empirical counterpart (X').

Just as we can conceive of a purely conceptual typology (X) with no empirical representation, we can alternatively conceive of a purely empirical taxonomy (X') with no theoretical counterpart. How could such a purely empirical taxonomy be constructed? We will answer this question in Chapter 3, in our discussion of cluster analysis. The basic strategy is simply to measure the empirical cases and group them by similarity. As a simplistic example, we could begin with a group of mixed black and white beans, and then group the black beans into one cluster and the white ones into another. These would be empirically derived classes (X') that might have little or no real theoretical value or conceptual importance.

These two examples represent the traditional theoretical and empirical levels of analysis. What is left that we can use to constitute the third level (X")? Upon reflection it becomes clear that there is a distinct third level that is common in everyday usage. This is the operational or indicator level (X"), and is formed by mapping both the conceptual (X) and empirical (X') levels into the third level (X"). Thus, the indicator level can be seen as a combination of the conceptual and empirical levels, and this explains why it is so frequently confused with, or merged with, one of these other levels. There are two basic types of indicator level (X") classification. One results from the common practice in social research of

32

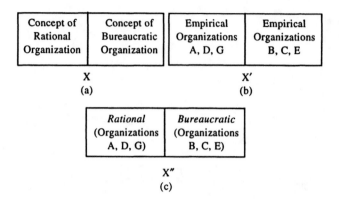

Concept of Rational Organization	Concept of Bureaucratic Organization	Empirical Organizations A, D, G	Empirical Organizations B, C, E

X
(a)

X'
(b)

Rational (Organizations A, D, G)	Bureaucratic (Organizations B, C, E)

X"
(c)

Figure 2.2. Illustration of: (a) Conceptual; (b) Empirical; and (c) Indicator-Level Classifications

first specifying concepts (X) and then subsequently measuring empirical examples (X') of these. An example would be where we first constructed a purely conceptual typology (X) as in Tables 1.1 and 2.1, and then identified empirical cases (X') for all or some of the cells. This strategy of forming a combined conceptual/empirical typology by first forming the concepts and then searching for empirical cases is what I have previously (Bailey, 1973) termed the *classical strategy*. This can be seen as a deductive strategy.

Indicator level (X") classifications can also be formed inductively, or by a strategy of "grounded theory" à la Glaser and Strauss (1967). This is the opposite strategy and consists of first forming empirical clusters (X'), and then subsequently formulating conceptual labels (X) for them. Whether one begins with theory or empirical data, when the two are combined the result is an operational or indicator level (X") classification. The three types of classifications, conceptual (X), empirical (X'), and the combined (operational or indicator) level (X") are shown in Figure 2.2.

Chapter 2 has been chiefly concerned with the first type of classification shown in Figure 2.2, the conceptual (X), but we have also discussed the third type, or indicator-level typologies (X"). We have discussed conceptual typologies in some detail, and have discussed indicator-level typologies chiefly in the form of classical typologies where empirical cases have been identified for the monothetic types. We have also discussed reduction, which either retains monotheticism (functional reduction) or results in polytheticism (pragmatic reduction or arbitrary numerical reduction).

Advantages and Disadvantages of Conceptual Typologies

The general advantages and disadvantages of classification were discussed in some detail in Chapter 1. Here it is appropriate to repeat some that particularly pertain to conceptual typologies, as well as adding some not mentioned in Chapter 1.

Advantages

1. Comparison. Despite the advent of computerization, conceptual criterion types remain the standard for comparison.

2. Heuristic Purposes. Typologies can be useful as heuristic devices to highlight the relevant theoretical dimensions of a type. In a real sense they are the premier tools for defining and explicating multidimensional type concepts.

3. Interaction Effects. A statistical interaction effect occurs when the effect of one variable on another is different depending upon the value of a third variable. As Stinchcombe (1968, pp. 46-47) has noted, typologies are useful in combining variables in such a way that interaction effects can be analyzed.

Drawing from Bailey (1992), I can summarize the merits of conceptual typologies in words somewhat different than used previously. To summarize, a well-constructed typology can be very effective in bringing order out of chaos. It can transform the complexity of apparently eclectic congeries of diverse cases into well-ordered sets of a few rather homogeneous types, clearly situated in a property space of a few important dimensions. A sound typology forms a solid foundation for both theorizing and empirical research. Perhaps no other tool has such power to simplify life for the social scientist.

Disadvantages

The chief disadvantages of classification in general have been discussed in Chapter 1, and the limitations specific to numerical taxonomy are discussed in Chapter 3. Thus we need not belabor a list of disadvantages here, but need only note in passing a summary of some criticisms (drawing again upon Bailey, 1992).

Some alleged weaknesses are that typologies (sometimes): are not mutually exclusive and exhaustive; are treated as ends in themselves, rather than as means to an end; are not sufficiently parsimonious; are based on arbitrary and ad hoc criteria; are essentially static; rely too much upon dichotomized variables rather than continuous variables; are subject to reification; and are descriptive rather than explanatory or predictive. Although some typology at some point in the past has doubtlessly been guilty of all these flaws, most of these ills are generally relatively easy for a knowledgeable typologist to avoid. The ones that cannot be easily avoided (such as reliance on static or cross-sectional data, or poor choice of variables) are usually seen to be general problems for social research as a whole and not specific to typology construction.

We are now ready to turn to a discussion of quantitative, empirical, cluster analysis. This can be identified in Figure 2.2 as our third type of classification to be discussed—empirical (X') classification. The construction of empirical taxonomies is generally accomplished through cluster analysis, or the various methods of numerical taxonomy. This is our topic in Chapter 3.

3. NUMERICAL TAXONOMY AND CLUSTER ANALYSIS

We have previously defined numerical taxonomy and cluster analysis. Chapter 3 is devoted to discussion of the various methods found within these rubrics. The monothetic typologies discussed in Chapter 2 are formed conceptually and deductively. Any empirical data, if utilized at all, enters the process relatively late, after the conceptual types have been formed. In cluster analysis the process is reversed. Here we begin with data, and seek to form our classification empirically, through numerical analysis of the empirical cases. Basically, cluster analysis seeks to group a sample of objects into homogeneous classes on the basis of their similarity on M variables.

Cluster analysis is now more than 50 years old. It was originated in psychology by Zubin (1938), and Tryon (1939), and in anthropology by Driver and Kroeber (1932). Computational complexity made clustering very difficult before the advent of computers. Computerization has led to a surge of developments since the late 1950s. Some of the notable references of interest to social scientists are the work of McQuitty (e.g.,

TABLE 3.1
The Score (S) Matrix of Objects and Variables

Objects	1	2	3				M
Jim	$Score_{11}$	$Score_{12}$	$Score_{13}$	•	•	•	$Score_{1M}$
Bill	$Score_{21}$	$Score_{22}$	$Score_{23}$	•	•	•	$Score_{2M}$
Jane	$Score_{31}$	$Score_{32}$	$Score_{33}$	•	•	•	$Score_{3M}$
•	•	•	•	•	•	•	•
•	•	•	•	•	•	•	•
•	•	•	•	•	•	•	•
O	$Score_{O1}$	$Score_{O2}$	$Score_{O3}$	•	•	•	$Score_{OM}$

1957, 1960, 1961, 1963), Bailey (1974, 1983, 1993), Capecchi (1966), Hudson and Associates (1982), and Lorr (1983). There is also a monograph in this series devoted entirely to cluster analysis (Aldenderfer & Blashfield, 1984). The standard references on numerical taxonomy include Anderberg (1973), Everitt (1980), Hartigan (1975), Johnson (1967), Jardine and Sibson (1971), Sneath and Sokal (1973), Sokal and Sneath (1963), Tversky (1977), and Wishart (1987).

The general procedure of cluster analysis is quite simple. We generally begin with a basic score matrix, as in Table 3.1. The score matrix (S-matrix) shows a set of scores for each of O objects (cases) on each of N variables. The idea is to group the most similar entities in this data matrix together. Thus, if the matrix contained data on 50 persons ($N = 50$), we might be able to cluster all 50 into three relatively homogeneous groups (e.g., one group of 16 persons, one group of 19 persons, and one group of 15 persons). Looking at Table 3.1, how can we group cases by similarity? The usual procedure is to choose one of two alternatives: either (1) compute measures of similarity (such as a correlation coefficient) or (2) compute measures of dissimilarity (such as distance measures) for all cases. The first alternative, computation of similarity measures, is probably most familiar to social scientists. Familiar measures of similarity include measures of association (for dichotomous data), or measures of correlation. Measures of dissimilarity or distance are less familiar.

The difference between similarity coefficients and dissimilarity (distance) coefficients is made clear in Figure 3.1. This figure shows the position of four individuals in a two-variable property space composed of variable 1 and variable 2. It is clear from visual inspection that individuals 1 and 2 would be grouped into cluster 1, and individuals 3 and 4 into cluster 2. In terms of similarity or dissimilarity, individuals 1 and 2 have

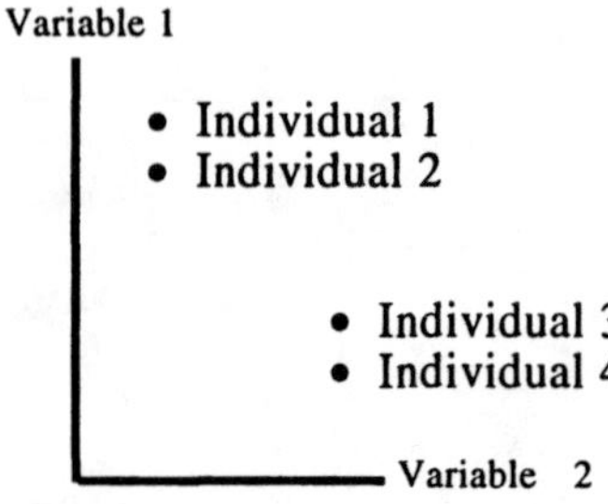

Variable 1

Figure 3.1. Illustration of Distance and Similarity Among Four Individuals in a Two-Variable Property Space
SOURCE: Bailey (1972). Reprinted by permission from Jossey-Bass, Inc.

high correlations (low distance) between each other, as do individuals 3 and 4. Comparing individuals 2 and 3, however, we see that they are quite dissimilar (exhibiting higher distance between them) on both variable 1 and variable 2, showing that their correlation is low. Thus, individuals close together in the property space show low distance (high correlation) on all dimensions, while those far apart show high distance (low correlation). This means that distance and correlation measures are the inverse of one another.

The type of coefficient to be used can also depend on the level of measurement or how the variables are coded. If the variables are continuously measured, a common measure of distance is:

$$D^2 = \sum_{i=1}^{K} (X_{A_i} - X_{B_i})^2$$

Here D is distance, K is the number of variables (dimensions), X_{A_i} signifies the value of variable i for object A, and X_{B_i} signifies the value of variable i for object B. An advantage of distance measures compared to correlation measures is that distance has an absolute zero point. That is, the only way that D (or D^2) can be zero is if the two objects are identical in value on all variables, thus both being at exactly the same location in the property space. Negative distance is undefined. As D_{AB} gets larger in a given property space, this signifies that A and B are farther apart on one or more variables.

If one decides to use a measure of similarity rather than distance, one popular measure is the well-known Pearson's r. Because r can only be

TABLE 3.2
Fourfold Table for Computation of Coefficients of Association

		Object i		
		1	0	
Object j	1	n_{11}	n_{01}	$n_{.1}$
	0	n_{10}	n_{00}	$n_{.0}$
		$n_{1.}$	$n_{0.}$	

SOURCE: Bailey (1974). Reprinted by permission from Jossey-Bass, Inc.

used for continuous data (interval or ratio), or rho for ordinal data, measures of association must be used if a similarity measure is desired for dichotomous or categorical data. These are also called nonparametric measures. Assume that we have a table as shown in Table 3.2. Cell 1 of Table 3.1 (n_{11}) shows the number of variables possessed by both objects (positive matches) while cell 4 (n_{00}) shows the number of variables not possessed by either object (negative matches). Cell 2 shows the number of variables possessed only by object j (n_{01}), while cell 3 shows the number possessed only by object i (n_{10}). The problem with negative matches (cell 4) is that here the two objects are similar only because they each lack some variable. Thus, you and your friend could be coded as similar because you both lack wings (or antlers).

The most straightforward measure of association is called the simple matching coefficient, or SMC (see Sokal & Sneath, 1963, p. 133).

$$SMC = (n_{11} + n_{00}) / N = (n_{11} + n_{00}) / (n_{10} + n_{01} + n_{11} + n_{00}).$$

For N cases it is just the sum of all positive and negative matches between two objects, expressed as a proportion of the total N. The SMC varies between 0 (no matches) and 1 (when there are only matches, or when the unmatched cells, cells 2 and 3, each have cell frequencies of zero). If you wish to exclude negative matches, simply remove the n_{00} term from both the numerator and denominator. This coefficient also varies between 0 (no positive matches) and 1 (when the cell frequency of both cells 2 and 3 is zero), and is called Jaccard's coefficient (Sokal & Sneath, 1963, p. 133).

There are also some coefficients of association that vary between -1 and $+1$. Two that are quite well known to social scientists are Yule's Q (the fourfold version of gamma), and phi (the fourfold version of r). Both of these are -1 when the number of positive matches (n_{11}) or negative matches (n_{00}) is 0. They are $+1$ when either of the unmatched terms $(n_{10}$ or $n_{01})$ is 0. They are both zero when the product of the matched pairs (both positive and negative matches) equals the product of the unmatched pairs.

$$\text{Yule's } Q = (n_{11}n_{00} - n_{10}n_{01}) \,/\, (n_{11}n_{00} + n_{10}n_{01})$$

$$\text{Phi} = (n_{11}n_{00} - n_{10}n_{01}) \,/\, (n_{1.}n_{0.}n_{.1}n_{.0})$$

Q and R Correlations

In addition to deciding whether to use distance or similarity coefficients, the cluster analyst also must decide whether to cluster objects (such as individuals) or variables (but generally not both simultaneously). Returning to the score matrix (Table 3.1), one has the choice of correlating pairs of variables (columns) or pairs of objects (rows). The internal data remain the same; it is merely a question of whether you correlate vertically or horizontally.

The standard practice in social science is to correlate vertically (to correlate variables). This is called R-analysis. It is also possible, however, to correlate horizontally (correlate objects). This is called Q-analysis. Our hypotheses generally refer to pairs of variables (such as referring to a positive relationship between education and income). Here, R-analysis is the preferred choice. For cluster analysis, however, we often are not interested in grouping variables into clusters or in writing hypotheses that link variables. Rather, we are more interested in grouping objects, such as individual persons. Thus we would rather construct clusters of objects (persons) on the basis of their similarity on the variables. This requires correlations among objects, or Q-correlation. Table 3.3 (from Stephenson, 1953, p. 169) shows Q-correlations among 15 persons measured on 121 variables (with decimal points omitted).

Persons unfamiliar with Q-analysis are often uneasy with the notion of correlating persons. But to repeat, the internal data are the same for either R- or Q-analysis. The only difference lies in the direction of the correlation procedures for the two techniques, which is equivalent to transposing the matrix of Table 3.1.

TABLE 3.3

Q-Correlations (Decimal Points Omitted) Among 15 Persons Measured on 121 Variables

	A	B	C	D	E	F	G	H	I	J	K	L	M	N	O
A	—	387	459	577	376	352	264	503	088	096	085	030	-005	023	030
B	387	—	603	493	242	431	307	392	-017	174	114	-006	049	082	159
C	459	603	—	615	463	508	399	522	-006	105	095	-043	080	094	099
D	577	493	615	—	398	572	441	607	087	083	138	062	100	172	063
E	376	242	463	398	—	557	320	500	137	190	148	107	077	140	172
F	352	431	508	572	557	—	324	467	095	089	128	013	044	015	101
G	264	307	399	441	320	324	—	370	-250	090	-040	-015	007	108	084
H	503	392	522	607	500	467	370	—	073	055	003	060	103	081	105
I	088	-017	-006	087	137	095	-250	073	—	357	365	251	208	197	324
J	096	174	105	083	190	089	090	055	357	—	392	409	483	392	580
K	085	114	095	138	148	128	-040	003	365	392	—	380	390	275	396
L	030	-006	-043	062	107	013	-015	060	251	409	380	—	353	333	400
M	-005	049	080	100	077	044	007	103	208	483	390	353	—	375	428
N	023	082	094	172	140	015	108	081	197	392	275	333	375	—	389
O	030	159	099	063	172	101	084	105	324	580	396	400	428	389	—

SOURCE: Reprinted from W. Stephenson (1953) *The Study of Behavior* (p. 169). Chicago: University of Chicago Press. Used by permission of the publisher.

Although the internal data in Table 3.1 are the same for Q-analysis as for R-analysis, however, social scientists often have more problems with Q-analysis than just the problem of deciding what it really means to correlate persons. Another problem is that while we can use sampling theory to derive a random sample of N persons from a population of persons, it is difficult to derive a random sample of M variables. This is because we generally do not know how to define a population or universe of variables from which to draw our sample. A large number of variables can be defined, and we can assume that this constitutes a universe, but cannot really be sure. Another problem for Q-analysis is that we generally need several times as many variables as objects in order to avoid degree of freedom problems.

Criteria for Evaluating Clustering Methods

We have already discussed Q- versus R-analysis and distance versus similarity measures as two basic choices that the cluster analyst must make. Unfortunately, the complexity does not end here. I have identified 15 criteria on which clustering methods can be evaluated. These amount to choices that the researcher must make. These are derived from Bailey (1974, pp. 74-87). Also see Sneath and Sokal (1973, pp. 202-214).

Criterion 1: Agglomerative Versus Divisive. Beginning with a sample of N objects of cases (such as persons), there are two basic ways to view the clustering problem. One can view the sample as consisting of N separate clusters, and can successively combine and recombine (agglomerate) them into a smaller set of clusters. This is called the agglomerative strategy. Alternatively, one can view the set of N objects as initially comprising a single large cluster. Then the task is to divide or partition the N objects into smaller clusters. This is known as the divisive strategy.

Criterion 2: Monothetic Versus Polythetic. This distinction has already been discussed in some detail. Clustering methods can be classified by whether they yield monothetic or polythetic clusters. Nearly all clustering methods yield polythetic clusters, especially if the sample size is large, and many variables are used in the clustering. If one wants to construct monothetic classes, then the best strategy is to use the classical conceptual methods previously discussed. Anyone wanting to construct monothetic types through cluster analysis will find the task difficult. The best strategy would probably be to use a divisive technique and a single classification, such as two clusters grouped on one variable. Then it may be possible for all members of a cluster to be identical (monothetic). In complex cases, however, we will generally find the empirical world to be too imperfect to yield monothetic clusters. If the researcher has a polythetic (but not fully polythetic) group it can be made monothetic by simply removing all characters that vary. The two chief methods of constructing monothetic clusters are the methods of Lockhart and Hartman (1963) and Williams and Lambert (1959). For further discussion of these techniques see Bailey (1974, pp. 105-107), and Chapter 4.

Criterion 3: Natural Versus Artificial. One can distinguish between natural and artificial clusters. The underlying assumption of so-called natural clustering is that groups of homogeneous objects exist empirically or "naturally," and that the task of cluster analysis is to identify, replicate, or even "capture" these already existing clusters. In contrast, artificial clusters, though they may be relatively homogeneous, would have no natural empirical cohesion. Artificial clustering is generally purely descriptive and its chief goal is to condense a sample.

The notion of natural clustering has been criticized by Fleiss and Zubin (1969), who say that the procedure is inadequate, as no statistical or mathematical model of a cluster exists. Rather, a cluster is defined, de facto, by the algorithm specific to each clustering technique. In spite of the criticism, virtually all agglomerative and most divisive methods have the goal of seeking natural, underlying clusters. Few numerical taxonomists would claim that they are seeking artificial clusters. One salient exception is Mayer's (1971) divisive method designed to create artificial clusters.

Criterion 4: Number of Clusters Predetermined or Not. You should be able to see the relationship between this criterion and Criterion 3. Theoretically, if clusters were purely artificial, then their number might also be artificial or arbitrary, allowing the researcher to set the number of clusters at will before beginning the clustering process. Because most researchers seek to identify preexisting natural clusters, however, they do not specify a number of clusters, but simply allow the data to determine them (they leave the determination of the number of clusters to "nature"). Thus most agglomerative methods do not predetermine the number of groups or clusters. Some divisive methods do prespecify the number of groups, usually only two or three for simplicity. Such prespecification greatly simplifies computational analysis, but also reduces the possibility of finding natural groupings (unless, of course, we somehow know the number of groups in advance). For further discussion of determining the number of clusters, see Aldenderfer and Blashfield (1984).

Criterion 5: Single Level Versus Hierarchical. Some clustering techniques yield clusters on a single level. One example is McQuitty's (1957) typal analysis. However, most commonly used agglomerative methods are hierarchical. Hierarchical methods involve successive clustering and reclustering (either agglomerative or divisive). In agglomerative hierarchical clustering, the N objects are first combined into N_1 clusters (e.g., 50 objects combined into 10 clusters). Next, these 10 clusters are recombined into N_2 (e.g., 6) larger clusters. Then these could be again recombined into N_3 (e.g., 2) still larger clusters. Divisive hierarchical methods also recluster, but from the opposite direction (from "above"). For example, the sample of N cases is first divided into two clusters; then these two are divided into four; then these four into eight; and so forth. For an example of a divisive hierarchical method see Edwards and Cavalli-Sforza (1965).

One common technique often encountered in cluster analysis is the hierarchical agglomerative method utilizing similarity (rather than distance) coefficients. Such methods are conveniently represented in tree graphs called dendograms (Sokal & Sneath, 1963, p. 27). A hypothetical dendogram is shown in Figure 3.2. The vertical lines attached to the horizontal lines are called stems. Figure 3.2 provides a graphical illustration of a level at which objects join to form initial clusters, and the levels at which these clusters successively rejoin or recluster. For example, in Figure 3.2, A and E join to form a cluster at a similarity level of .90 (the highest correlation in the matrix), while C and F join at .80. Object B joins the first cluster (A and E) at .80, while D joins Cluster 2 (C and F) at .70. The two clusters would coalesce at .20.

Criterion 6: Overlapping Versus Nonoverlapping. Since most clustering (particularly agglomerative clustering) attempts to construct naturally occurring empirical taxonomies, the resulting taxa must follow the classic rules of typology construction. This means that clusters must be mutually exclusive and exhaustive, as discussed previously. Every empirical case must fit into one (but only one) cluster. Thus, clusters cannot overlap. The result is that most clustering methods are nonoverlapping. When research goals can accommodate overlapping clusters, however, this can greatly facilitate the clustering procedure. The maximization of cluster homoge-

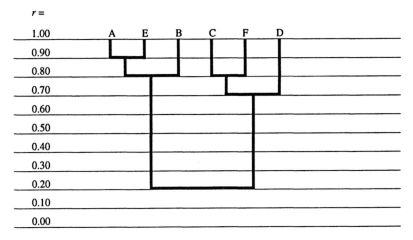

Figure 3.2. Dendrogram Showing a Hypothetical Tree
SOURCE: Bailey (1974). Reprinted by permission from Jossey-Bass, Inc.

neity may be enhanced through overlapping methods, as this allows an object that is intermediate between two clusters to be placed in both. Probably the most popular overlapping technique is Needham's (1961) "clumping" technique, but McQuitty (1956) and others have also devised overlapping techniques.

Criterion 7: Outliers Permitted or Not. An outlier is a single object without a cluster. The existence of many outliers can be a real problem for clustering. If a single case lies far from a cluster, there are a number of strategies that can be used. One is simply to let it remain as an unclustered outlier. Another is to remove it from the sample (and thus from the cluster analysis). A third strategy is to include it in the cluster with which it fits best, but this may damage the internal homogeneity of the cluster by relaxing the usual rules for clustering.

Which of these is preferred may depend both on the theoretical and research goals and on the particular clustering technique utilized. Theoretically, leaving outliers violates the typological requirement of exhaustiveness. One way around this is simply to consider each outlier as constituting its own cluster, but this frequently leads to an unacceptable and nonparsimonious number of clusters. The issue is more serious for agglomerative methods, as most divisive methods, by partitioning the set, include all cases on one side or another of the boundary and so do not leave outliers (although they may yield heterogeneous clusters). Agglomerative methods are more problematic because they begin with all cases essentially as outliers, and a case remains an outlier until clustered. The agglomerative methods that we will discuss shortly as "objective" rather than "subjective" methods are less likely to leave outliers, because each case is admitted to the cluster that it has its highest similarity level with, even if this similarity level is low.

Subjective methods, in which the researcher sets the level for admittance of a case to a cluster, may leave more outliers if the researcher insists on similarity levels that are unrealistically high for the given data set. That is, if object 12 has a correlation of .25 with an object in Cluster 1, and a correlation of .21 with an object in Cluster 2, it will remain an outlier if the researcher requires an admittance similarity level of .30 or more. If the researcher drops the minimum level to .25, however, then object 12 can join Cluster 1 and is no longer an outlier.

Criterion 8: Form of Linkage—Single, Average, Complete. A very critical decision that every cluster analyst must make when using agglomerative methods regards the form of linkage between a potential candidate for a cluster and the cluster. Assume that you are using Pearson's *r* as a similarity coefficient, and have a cluster under construction that now contains three objects: A, B, and C. The question is whether object D is qualified to join that cluster. If not, it either may join another cluster or remain as an outlier (unclustered). There are many criteria that could be formulated as admittance rules, but only three basic ones that are commonly used in agglomerative clustering methods. These are single linkage, average linkage, and complete linkage.

By the single linkage criterion, an object is admitted to a cluster if it has a correlation with only a single member of that cluster that is higher than its correlation with any object not in the cluster. By this criterion, a cluster is a group in which each member of the group is more like at least one other member of the group than it is like any object not in the group.

In complete linkage methods, it is not sufficient for a prospective member to be highly correlated with only a single member of the cluster. Here, an object can be admitted to a cluster only if it is more highly correlated with every member of the cluster than with any object not in the cluster. Clusters formed by complete linkage methods are more compact than those formed by single linkage methods, which tend to be more chain-like.

The third form of linkage, average linkage analysis, is intermediate to the other two forms. In average linkage analysis, objects are admitted to clusters only if they do not lower the average similarity level of that cluster by more than a predetermined amount.

Single linkage methods may be too simplistic and not sufficiently rigorous. By requiring a link with only one object, they may be "space-expanding," and yield heterogeneous or even overlapping clusters. They are sometimes referred to as "nearest neighbor" methods. This is a reference to the position of the objects in the property space. In single linkage methods, an object joins the cluster of its nearest neighbor, or the object that it is closest to in the property space. Single linkage methods may be adequate if the objects are naturally arranged in a chain-like fashion, but may be less adequate for other types of naturally occurring clusters.

In contrast, complete linkage methods are space contracting, in that they yield tight, homogeneous clusters. They are often referred to as "farthest neighbor" or "furthest neighbor" methods (see Bailey, 1974, p. 101). Again, the analogy is to position in a property space. In a complete linkage method, we are most concerned with how the prospective member of a cluster relates to its farthest neighbor in the cluster. It must be closer to its farthest neighbor in the cluster than to all objects in all other clusters, if it is to be admitted to the cluster. Farthest neighbor methods also maximize the distance between objects that are members of two different groups. To summarize, in farthest neighbor (complete linkage) methods, distance between two clusters is measured between the two most distant individuals in the two clusters; while in the nearest neighbor (single linkage) methods, distance between two clusters is measured between the two nearest individuals, one in each cluster.

Criterion 9: Objective Versus Subjective Similarity Level. As with numerous other decisions in cluster analysis, the researcher must decide whether the similarity or (dissimilarity) level will be objectively or subjectively set. In a subjective method, the researcher subjectively determines the level of similarity at which a prospective member will enter a cluster. These levels may be set arbitrarily, or by experience, or by perusal of the data to determine the apparently best levels, or for theoretical or other reasons. In any event, the researcher must determine the level to be used, and preset it, before clustering can commence.

In an objective method, the researcher has no such decision to make. Here the researcher simply utilizes the highest similarity level (or lowest dissimilarity level) in the matrix, thus yielding maximum homogeneity for the cluster. To illustrate both objective and subjective levels, suppose that we have formed the nucleus of Cluster 1 with objects A and B. Suppose also that researcher Smith chooses a subjectively set level of .90 as the minimum acceptable similarity level for a new object to enter a cluster, while researcher Jones uses objectively set levels. Suppose we find that object C correlates .75 with object B, and that this is the highest remaining correlation in the matrix. That is, C does not correlate higher with any other object, and no other two objects have higher correlations than .75. This means that C cannot enter the cluster by Smith's criterion, because .75 is less than .90. It does enter by Jones's, however, because objective similarity admits at the highest level in the matrix, which in this case is .75.

Criterion 10: Combinatorial Versus Noncombinatorial. This distinction was formulated by Lance and Williams (1967). In combinatorial methods, all measures used during the successive stages of the clustering can be computed from measures used previously. For example, if distance coefficients are computed from the score matrix of Table 3.1, then combinatorial methods use only the distance measures. In contrast, noncombinatorial methods would require the investigator to return to the original matrix of Table 3.1 for recomputation of measures during later stages of the clustering process. Thus, the original matrix of Table 3.1 would have to be retained throughout the analysis.

Criterion 11: Compatible Versus Incompatible. This distinction is similar to Criterion 10 and was also devised by Lance and Williams (1967). In a compatible clustering method, measures calculated later in the analysis are the same kind as measures calculated earlier. In contrast, an incompatible method is one in which some properties of the original measure (either similarity or dissimilarity) are lost during the course of the analysis, causing problems in interpretation.

Incompatibility generally arises when the clustering method begins by computing similarity or distance measures between individuals, and then switches over to the computation of similarity or distance between clusters, rather than individuals. Sometimes, whether a method is compatible or incompatible depends upon which measures are used; for example, being incompatible only with correlation coefficients or information measures (Bailey, 1974, p. 84). Fortunately, most commonly used methods are compatible.

Criterion 12: Iterative Versus Noniterative. Another criterion is whether the computational method is iterative or not. The early clustering methods were all noniterative. Now, however, a number of iterative methods exist in which a cluster is continuously improved in successive stages of computation. Some of the best known iterative methods are discussed by Ball (1965) and Friedman and Rubin (1967).

Criterion 13: Sequential Versus Simultaneous Methods. As distinguished by Sneath and Sokal (1973, pp. 208-209), this criterion differentiates sequential from nonsequential methods. In sequential methods, clustering proceeds in a series or sequence of steps, rather than in a single operation. That is, in sequential methods, clusters are formed rather slowly, one step at a time, by sequentially adding new members. In contrast, simultaneous or nonsequential methods form all clusters—and thus cluster all objects—simultaneously, in one step. Almost all commonly used agglomerative techniques are sequential. However, some simple divisive techniques may cluster simultaneously. For further discussion of simultaneous procedures see Sneath and Sokal (1973, pp. 208-209).

Criterion 14: Local Versus Global. This criterion was also formulated by Sneath and Sokal (1973, p. 209). *Local versus global* refers to the degree of reliability with which the distances between objects in the input matrix are maintained. In hierarchical methods, clustering solutions are often not uniformly good at all levels of the hierarchy. For example, if a method can uniformly yield "tight" or homogeneous clusters at all hierarchical levels, or in all regions of the property space, then it is said to be a global method, or have global reliability. A nonuniform method, for example, may reliably estimate similarities among objects within a cluster, but become increasingly unreliable as larger clusters are considered. This would be labeled a local method. For further discussion see Sneath and Sokal (1973, p. 209).

Criterion 15: Weighted Versus Nonweighted Clustering. Weighted versus nonweighted clustering was also contributed by Sneath and Sokal (1973, pp. 211-212). There are various forms of weighting that can be done, such as considering some variables as more important (e.g., multiplying their values by two) than other variables. Some critics see any such weighting as inherently arbitrary. Sneath and Sokal (1973, p. 212) note, however, that in a sense all procedures are weighted because a researcher who fails to weight some variables more than others is really weighting (perhaps arbitrarily) all of them the same (is de facto multiplying them all by one). Regardless of this claim of equal weighting, it still seems to me that unequal weighting should be done very carefully and only for good theoretical or empirical reasons.

Although a large number of criteria have been discussed, not all of them will be encountered equally frequently by cluster analysts. In fact the most frequently used methods for empirical taxonomic work in biological and social science are agglomerative methods. Of these, the most frequently used are a subset of agglomerative methods for which Sneath and Sokal (1973) used the acronym SAHN. The term SAHN stands for sequential, agglomerative, hierarchical, nonoverlapping clustering methods. To be even more specific, although all of these criteria are important in certain instances, the criteria we will rely on the most in this chapter include Criterion 1 (agglomerative vs. divisive), Criterion 2 (monothetic vs. polythetic), Criterion 5 (single level vs. hierarchical), Criterion 8 (form of linkage—single, average, or complete), and Criterion 9 (objective vs. subjective similarity level). For further discussion of these and other criteria, please see Bailey (1974) and Sneath and Sokal (1973).

A Typology of Clustering Techniques

One difficulty with discussing individual clustering methods is that so many different ones have been devised that it is virtually impossible adequately to discuss them all. They are so disparate, and vary on so many dimensions, that it is sometimes difficult to classify or even summarize them. As Sneath and Sokal say:

> The difficulty of outlining the major kinds of approaches to clustering biological data is compounded by the inability of workers in the field to arrive at a logical system of classification of clustering methods. . . . There seems to be no way of erecting a consistent system of clustering algorithms. Binary division of the eight different aspects would lead to $2^8 = 256$ types of clustering methods. (1973, p. 202)

Although Sneath and Sokal discussed only eight criteria for classifying clusters, I identified 15. Thus, a full typology devised from dichotomizing my 15 characteristics would lead to $2^{15} = 32,768$ types. Obviously, this would be far too unwieldy to be of much use. Fortunately, however, the situation is not quite as bleak as Sneath and Sokal would make it seem.

TABLE 3.4
Typology of Clustering Methods

| | | Form of Linkage | |
	Single	Average	Complete
Subjective	Elementary cluster analysis Sneath's method (1957) Method of Sawrey, Keller, and Conger (1960) Method of Zubin, Fleiss, and Burdock (1963) Bailey's (1974, 1993) method	Sokal and Michener's (1958) weighted-variable-group method Sokal and Michener's (1958) weighted-pair-group method Centroid method Median method	Sørensen's (1948) method
Type of Similarity Level	1	2	3
Objective	McQuitty's (1957) elementary linkage analysis McQuitty's (1957) hierarchical analysis Nearest-neighbor method	Method of Edwards and Cavalli-Sforza (1965) Method of Friedman and Rubin (1967) MacQueen's (1967) method McRae's (1971) method Forgy's (1965) method 5a – – – – – – – – – – Method of Williams, Lambert, and Lance (1966) Ward's (1963) method 5b	McQuitty's (1963, 1965) typal analysis Method of Saunders and Schucman (see Fleiss & Zubin, 1969)
	4		6

SOURCE: Bailey (1974). Reprinted by permission from Jossey-Bass, Inc.

The vast majority of popular clustering methods can be accommodated in a typology of only two dimensions, as shown in Table 3.4. The methods in cells 1, 2, 3, 4, 5, 6 are all agglomerative. Many of them are SAHN methods, although some are not, such as McQuitty's (1957) typal analysis. The divisive methods are confined to cell 5a. The typology in Table 3.4 is formed from only 2 of the 15 criteria (Criterion 8, form of linkage, and

Criterion 9, objective vs. subjective similarity level). These two criteria were selected because they are so central to all agglomerative methods. They also offer the most variability, while some of the other criteria are constant over a large number of methods and so really do not distinguish well among most methods. The methods illustrated in Table 3.4 are not intended to be exhaustive of all extant clustering methods. They are an arbitrary cross-section of methods and were selected for their utility and computational ease, and to provide examples for all cells.

Examples of Clustering

Although it is impossible to provide worked examples of all of the many clustering techniques that have been devised, we can select one or a few techniques from each of the cells of Table 3.4 and illustrate how these techniques are utilized. We will apply these various techniques to the Q-correlations of Table 3.3. These Q-correlations were computed by Stephenson (1953) on the basis of responses from 15 persons to 121 introversion-extroversion items. The degree of homogeneity exhibited in this matrix is quite high, and the matrix yields very illustrative clusters.

Remember that we need not use similarity coefficients such as the Q-correlations of Table 3.3 for clustering, but could instead utilize distance measures computed either between variables or between objects. The Q-correlations of Table 3.3 are used for illustrative purposes only, and the reader should not infer that such Q-measures are necessarily superior over either R-similarity measures or distance measures for cluster applications. The choice of the coefficient will depend upon theoretical and empirical considerations, among other things, in any given research application.

Before examining specific techniques, let us peruse Table 3.3. The idea is to find clusters that exist empirically in this data set. Since we desire homogeneous "natural" taxa, the clusters should be "tight," exhibiting as little internal variability as possible. Further, since we desire nonoverlapping clusters, the clusters should be as separate from each other as possible. Returning to Table 3.4, let us first examine some subjective methods (cells 1, 2, and 3).

Subjective Similarity Level

Single Linkage. One of the simplest clustering techniques is a single linkage, subjective method from cell 1 of Table 3.4, named elementary cluster analysis (Sokal & Sneath, 1963, p. 179). All that is necessary is for a researcher to arbitrarily set a subjective similarity level and see what clusters are found (by single linkage) at that level. Let us arbitrarily set a similarity level of 700. We see that this will not work, as no objects are related this strongly. Reducing the level to 600, we see that $r_{CD} = 615$. Are there any other objects that link with either C or D (remember this is single linkage) at the 600 level or above? Searching the matrix, we see that H links with D at the required level ($r_{DH} = 607$), and also that B links with C ($r_{BC} = 603$). Thus, we so far have an incipient cluster of B, C, D, H. There are not any other links at the 600 level, so let us arbitrarily reduce the similarity level needed for admittance to a cluster to 500. Are there any single linkages at this level? Perusing the remaining objects, we quickly see that A links with D ($r_{AD} = 577$); F also links with D ($r_{FD} = 572$) and this allows E to link with F ($r_{FE} = 557$). This so far gives us a cluster of A, B, C, D, E, F, and H.

Examination of Table 3.3 shows that $r_{JO} = 580$. Thus, J and O form the nucleus of a second cluster. Are there any other remaining objects that link more closely with these two than with any other clusters? There are not at the 500 level, but moving to the 400 level, we see that L and M both join Cluster 2 ($r_{MJ} = 483$ and $r_{LJ} = 409$). Also, G now links with Cluster 1 ($r_{GD} = 441$) to complete this cluster. What about the three remaining objects, I, K, and N? They cannot link at the 400 level, but by lowering the required level to 300, we see that all three link with Cluster 2. This completes our cluster analysis, with two mutually exclusive and exhaustive clusters (and no outliers). Cluster 1 contains A, B, C, D, E, F, G, H, and Cluster 2 contains I, J, K, L, M, N, O.

Single linkage methods are often called "nearest neighbor methods" because a prospective member of a cluster need only link with its nearest neighbor in the property space in order to join the cluster (see McKelvey, 1982, p. 401). They are also called "space-contracting methods," as they may join relatively dissimilar objects (and so "contract" space) by virtue of a single link between two objects. That is, an object may be similar to one object in a cluster, and thus join that cluster, but be very dissimilar to other objects in the cluster.

In contrast, complete linkage methods (discussed later in this chapter) are often termed "furthest neighbor" or "farthest neighbor" methods, as here a prospective member of a cluster is compared to the member of an existing cluster that is farthest from it, and must link with that member as well before it can be admitted to the cluster. Single linkage methods are really very simple and exhibit flaws that have caused them to be labeled as inadequate, least adequate, or even obsolete (see McKelvey, 1982, p. 403).

The chief problem with elementary cluster analysis is that it does not always yield nonoverlapping clusters as it did here. Often, we will have outliers unless the admittance criterion is lowered to a very low level, at which point a single object can often join two clusters simultaneously, thus resulting in cluster overlap. Thus, with high similarity levels the method leaves outliers (thus violating the principle of exhaustivity), while at low similarity levels it permits cluster overlap (thus violating the principle of mutual exclusivity). This overlap problem renders elementary cluster analysis generally unsuitable for constructing empirical taxonomies.

Fortunately, there is a rather simple mechanism for avoiding the pernicious problem of cluster overlap. This is simply first to form a nucleus for the agglomerative cluster and then to successively add members to this nucleus, rather than forming the whole cluster simultaneously, as we did in elementary cluster analysis. Elsewhere (Bailey, 1993) I have discussed this matter of nucleus formation at length. The four principal choices are shown in Table 3.5. These four choices are formed from two dimensions. One is the familiar subjective-objective choice. The other is what I have termed "within versus between." We wish to minimize within-group heterogeneity, while maximizing between-group heterogeneity. To accomplish the former, we can choose as a nucleus the two most similar individuals in the matrix. To accomplish the latter, we can choose the two most dissimilar (distant) individual objects in the matrix to simultaneously form the nuclei for two separate clusters. This effectively minimizes the chance of cluster overlap.

It turns out that most extant SAHN methods use as a nucleus the largest reciprocal pair (the largest coefficient in the matrix). Sneath's (1957) method also utilizes this strategy. The simplest way to find the reciprocal pair is to search each column of Table 3.3 and circle the largest coefficient, which in Table 3.3 is $r_{CD} = 615$. Also, as each new object is added to the cluster, its column can be marked from the matrix (as we would now mark out columns C and D) so it is easy to determine which objects remain in the matrix as candidates to be admitted to clusters.

From this point on, Sneath's method, which is a subjective, single linkage method, successively lowers the admission level by equal amounts. Let us arbitrarily choose 050 as the increment to be lowered each time. Searching at a level 050 below the reciprocal pair (565) for single linkages to either C or D, we find H ($r_{HD} = 607$), B ($r_{BC} = 603$), F ($r_{FD} = 572$), and

TABLE 3.5
Typology of Nucleus Formation

	Within	Between
Objective	Sneath (1957)	Zubin, Fleiss, and Burdock (1963)
Subjective	Sawrey, Keller, and Conger (1960)	Bailey (1974, 1993)

SOURCE: Bailey (1974). Reprinted by permission from Jossey-Bass, Inc.

A (r_{AD} = 577). This level also begins a new cluster with J and O (the nucleus for Cluster 2). The 515 level admits E to Cluster 1 (r_{EF} = 557). The 465 level adds M to Cluster 2 (r_{MJ} = 483). The 415 level completes Cluster 1 by adding G to it (r_{GD} = 441). The 365 level completes Cluster 2 with L (r_{LJ} = 409), N (r_{NJ} = 392), K (r_{KJ} = 392), and I (r_{KI} = 365).

The method of Sawrey, Keller, and Conger (1960) is virtually the same as Sneath's, except that the nucleus link is subjectively chosen. Imagine that we set a level of 565 for beginning a cluster. This gives us A, B, C, D, F, and H as the large nucleus for Cluster 1, and J and O as the nucleus for Cluster 2. From here on, the method is identical to Sneath's.

Switching now to the method of Zubin, Fleiss, and Burdock (1963), we examine an objective "between" technique, where we look for the most dissimilar pair in the matrix and use each member of this pair as a nucleus for a separate cluster. This means that we must search Table 3.3 for negative correlations. The two most dissimilar persons are seen to be G and I (r_{GI} = –250). Using them as two simultaneous nuclei will give us two widely separated clusters, thus guarding against the problem of cluster overlap.

Logic, however, tells us that because G and I are the most distant persons in the entire matrix, their clusters must fall in between them in the property space, and this was demonstrated in our previous analysis, when G and I were the last persons admitted to their clusters (two different clusters). This method also adds members subjectively by single linkage. If we begin with a similarity level of 615 and lower the level 025 each time, we reach the 440 level for Cluster 1 and the 365 level for Cluster 2 before another member is admitted. After these key members are admitted, all other members of each cluster join simultaneously, as they all cluster with each other at higher levels.

The last subjective single linkage method to be discussed is Bailey's method (see Bailey, 1974, 1993). It is the same as the last method discussed, except that the dissimilar nuclei pairs are chosen subjectively, rather than objectively. The obvious problem with the method of Zubin et al. is that outliers are often chosen as nuclei. Thus one chooses nuclei that are not central to any cluster. A better way, as in Bailey's method, is often to eschew reliance on the most distant pair in favor of a pair that is somewhat nearer the middle. For example, rather than using the most dissimilar pair G and I as nuclei, one might achieve better clustering by choosing nuclei "in-between" these probable outliers. One way to accomplish this is to choose as the nucleus the variable that correlates most highly with each half of the dissimilar pair. For Cluster 1 this would yield D (correlating 441 with G) and for Cluster 2 this would yield K (correlating 365 with I). Although this method is certainly subjective compared to the method of Zubin et al., it is objective in the sense that one must seek only the highest link to each part of the dissimilar pair.

Let us pursue this strategy by subjectively choosing 025 as the criterion level to be lowered each time. Starting with the highest value in the matrix (615) we first lower this criterion 025 to 590. This adds both C and H to D (the nucleus of Cluster 1), and thus also adds B (which links with C). The next pass (565) adds A and F (linked with D). The next four levels (540, 515, 490, 465), do not add any objects, but the next one (440) adds G (linking with D). This completes Cluster 1. Cluster 2 is formed in a similar fashion and need not be illustrated here.

Notice that while all of the methods discussed so far yield the same two clusters, the dendograms for these methods (if drawn) can vary widely. This is because the methods vary in the number of objects entering a cluster at a given stage. Also notice that if we proceeded far enough in the analysis (which we did not do in any of the methods discussed), the two clusters would coalesce at the 190 similarity level (r_{EJ} =190).

Average Linkage. We are still discussing subjective methods, but turn now to the illustration of an average linkage method (cell 2 of Table 3.4). Average linkage methods, such as those by Sokal and Michener (1958), begin with a reciprocal pair as a nucleus (the coefficient that is the highest for both objects). The highest coefficient in the matrix is by definition a symmetrical (reciprocal) pair, and in Table 3.3 this is C and D (r_{CD} = 615). Average linkage is the same as single linkage, except here the subjectively set level represents the maximum that the average correlation among members can be lowered. For example, if the subjective similarity level were set at 025, this would mean that an object could be added to the cluster only if the average correlation among all members of the cluster were not more than 025 lower after the object was added than before it was added. You can see that this method requires a lot more computation than the others just discussed, as average correlations for all members must be computed over and over as members are added. Such a method is thus greatly facilitated through computerization, and using it without the computer can become very tedious indeed.

Complete Linkage. An example of a subjective complete linkage agglomerative method is Sørensen's (1948) method (cell 3 of Table 3.4). Here again we begin with the highest reciprocal pair (C and D), which are correlated at 615. We can subjectively set 025 as the amount for lowering the level each cycle. Going 025 below 615, we search for coefficients of 590 or more. This time, however, a prospective member must be correlated this highly with all members already in the cluster (i.e., with both C and D). Thus, while B, F, and H form single linkages at this level, they do not meet the complete linkage criterion for membership. For example, one has to go all the way to the 515 level, when H joins, linking with its highest levels to both C and D ($r_{HC} = 522$; and $r_{HD} = 607$). Complete linkage methods produce tighter, more compact clusters than do single linkage methods, but generally require more cycles to complete these clusters, as the criteria for admission are more rigorous. Sørensen's method illustrates the furthest neighbor method (Jardine & Sibson, 1968, p. 178), because it maximizes the distance between objects that are members of two different groups.

Objective Similarity Level

The procedures for single, average, and complete linkage are essentially the same for objective as for subjective similarity. The only difference is that before (with subjective levels) the researcher was required to set levels of admittance to clusters. Now, with objective analysis, the researcher need not make decisions about admittance levels, but only need admit the objects that have the highest similarity (or lowest distance), whatever that may be, at each cycle.

Single Linkage. One simple single linkage, objective method is McQuitty's (1957) elementary linkage analysis (cell 4 of Table 3.4). As before, we begin the analysis with a reciprocal pair. As we have seen, the largest reciprocal pair is C and D ($r_{CD} = 615$). Now we simply look for any objects that have their highest (objective) correlation with either C or D (single linkage). Examination shows that A, B, F, G, and H all qualify. Now we can look for any remaining objects having their highest correlations with any of these objects just admitted. Object E enters ($r_{EF} = 557$). There are no other objects that have their highest correlations with E, so this cluster is completed.

The task now is simply to start over and treat the remaining objects in the matrix as a new clustering procedure. This is facilitated by simply marking out the rows and columns of the objects in Cluster 1 and beginning to construct Cluster 2. Doing this yourself as an exercise, you will quickly locate the remaining reciprocal pairs, J and O ($r_{JO} = 580$), and then see that the remaining objects link to either J or O objectively, at single linkage until Cluster 2 is also complete.

Complete Linkage. Complete linkage analysis is a direct extension of single linkage, as we have seen previously for subjective methods. Objective complete linkage analysis simply requires that every member of a cluster be more highly correlated with every other member of the same cluster than with any object not in the cluster. As before, one begins with the highest reciprocal pair (C and D) as the nucleus. Examples of objective complete linkage methods (cell 6 of Table 3.4) are McQuitty's (1963, 1965) rank order typal analysis, and the method of Saunders and Schucman (see Fleiss & Zubin, 1969). Computation of these techniques is a straightforward extension of the earlier techniques that we have worked, and we need not go through them all. For further discussion and examples of these techniques, please see Bailey (1974).

Average Linkage. The only remaining cell of Table 3.4 to be discussed is cell 5. Cell 5 contains both agglomerative, average linkage, objective methods (cell 5b) and divisive, average linkage, objective methods (cell 5a). We will first discuss the agglomerative methods of cell 5b, then end our discussion by returning to cell 5a of Table 3.4 to analyze the various divisive techniques. The problem with average linkage objective methods is that they can require a great deal of computation. The basic criterion for admission is that the average similarity of the cluster be maximized. This can thus require computing the similarity level for all members and each prospective member, to determine which one of all the prospective members promises the highest average similarity level. For example, C and D can enter a cluster, as they clearly have the highest similarity level in the matrix. But in order to add a new object, the average similarity level among C, D, and all 13 remaining objects must be computed to see which is the highest. Thus, objective average linkage methods require a great deal of computation, and for this reason most of them are computerized. Because they are computerized, I cannot illustrate a simple worked example, but will briefly describe the methods shown in cell 5 of Table 3.4.

One popular agglomerative, objective, average linkage technique is Ward's (1963) hierarchical clustering method. This method begins with each object treated as a cluster of one. Then objects are successively combined. The criterion for combination is that the within-cluster variation as measured by the sum of within-cluster deviation from cluster means (error sum of squares) is minimized. Thus, the average distances among all members of the cluster are minimized.

One of the original clustering methods, and one now available in a computerized version, is also an objective, agglomerative, average linkage method. This is Tryon's (1939, 1955; Tryon & Bailey, 1970) method. This method uses Holzinger's (1937) *B* coefficient, which is a ratio of the average correlation of objects in a cluster to the average correlation of all objects not in the cluster. The object is to maximize *B*.

Divisive Methods

As contrasted with "bottom up" agglomerative methods, divisive methods are "top down." They begin with the whole sample in a single group and attempt to divide it into groups that are as internally homogeneous as possible. The major problem with most divisive methods is that they require a great deal of computation. Thus, most divisive methods were not invented until after computerization and virtually all divisive methods used now are computerized. Divisive methods are called "iterative partitioning methods" by Aldenderfer and Blashfield (1984).

Many divisive methods can be identified as average linkage methods with objectively set similarity levels. Their goal is easily stated: to divide the sample of objects into groups that display the greatest degree of within-group homogeneity. Although this task seems easy, there are two main problems confronting such divisive methods. One is that the number of partitions that must be executed before we can be sure that we have chosen the optimum partition is often prohibitive for even a moderately large sample. The other problem is that there is no currently accepted measure of homogeneity. The divisive problem would be simple if we could just examine all possible splits or partitions of the sample, until the best ones were found. The problem is that for a sample of size N, there are 2^{N-1} splits to be examined. Gower (1967) notes that for a sample of only size $N = 41$, this would take more than 54,000 years of computer time. Obviously this direct approach is out of the question, so an approximation algorithm of some sort must be devised.

But apart from the computational difficulties, users of divisive methods face a dilemma in trying to draw cluster boundaries around the proper set of objects. The problem in the univariate case is that we wish to minimize the variance for the cluster. We cannot compute the variance, however, until we have drawn the boundary (so we can compute the mean), but we cannot draw the boundary unless we know the variance, so we can minimize it. Even if we could measure the variance, this becomes difficult in the multivariate case (the usual case), where we have many cluster means—one for each variable.

As a way around all of these problems, researchers have used various measures to gauge the internal homogeneity of clusters sought in divisive methods. For each partition of N objects into G groups, the following identity matrix can be defined:

$$T = W + B$$

where W is the pooled within-group scatter matrix and B is the between-group scatter matrix. For the univariate case, T is the total SS (sum of squares), while W is the within-SS and B is the between-SS. These are used often by social statisticians in the familiar F ratio.

There are several approaches that can be taken to minimize within-cluster homogeneity. Edwards and Cavalli-Sforza (1965) suggested minimizing W. When this is done, the distance between clusters is also maximized because total variance is fixed, thus B is also maximized. Friedman and Rubin (1967) suggested maximizing

$$T/W = 1 + B/W.$$

This maximizes the ratio B/W, thus maximizing the F ratio. Also, since T is a constant, this minimizes W. A third criterion used by Friedman and Rubin (1967) was the maximization of trace $W^{-1}B$. All of these criteria are highly related.

Once the criterion for measuring cluster homogeneity has been chosen, the strategy for divisive clustering is generally quite straightforward. One simply constructs a particular initial split of the sample into clusters, and measures the within-cluster homogeneity (using the chosen criterion) of each cluster. This initial partitioning may be a random or arbitrary split, or may be made by the researcher on the basis of advance knowledge about what might be the best split. After the initial split is made, the divisive method proceeds by simply trying to improve upon these clusters; for example, by iteratively improving them.

The initial partition is very important in divisive clustering. If a poor initial partition is made, it can result in objects being placed in the wrong cluster. If this is done early in the divisive clustering procedures, as a practical matter it sometimes becomes very difficult to detect it and to find a mechanism for moving objects to a better cluster. Thus a very bad initial split can often doom the entire clustering procedure, by moving objects far away from their optimal cluster.

We would hope, however, that while the initial split is in need of improvement, it is not poorly done. If the initial split is moderately successful, the subsequent modifications simply seek to refine and improve the clusters. There are a number of strategies for accomplishing this. Three strategies presented by Friedman and Rubin (1967) are the *hill-climbing pass, the forcing pass,* and *the reassignment pass.* The hill-climbing pass entails examination of each individual (object) to determine whether internal cluster homogeneity (as measured by the particular criterion the investigator has chosen) can be improved by moving the individual to another cluster (all other clusters must be examined). Forcing passes and reassignment passes have similar functions. They begin with the initial partition and then reassign some objects to other groups so that the object is nearest the group center of gravity, or centroid. Such centroid strategies are well known in divisive clustering and simply try to place all objects as near as possible to the group's center, or centroid (multivariate group mean). This in fact minimizes the internal variance of the cluster.

Perhaps the most famous centroid method is the K-means procedure. It is featured in CLUSTAN (Wishart, 1987). The initial partitioning of the data is done in CLUSTAN by arbitrarily assigning the cases into K clusters (the user specifies the value of K). Then, Euclidian distances are computed between all objects and the K-cluster centroids, with each case being assigned to the cluster with the nearest centroid. After these reassignments, new centroids are computed, and the process begins all over again and is done over and over (iteratively), with continued improvement in the clusters. This "nearest centroid" pass is referred to as either the "reassignment pass" or the "K-means pass." For further information see Aldenderfer and Blashfield (1984, pp. 45-49).

These divisive methods can all be recognized as objective average linkage methods. They are objective, because they seek to maximize the criterion, rather than requiring the investigator to set an arbitrary, subjective level. They are average linkage methods because the within, between, and total SS of distances represent averages computed by summing across objects in the sample. For other well-known strategies to improve partitions after the initial one, see Forgy (1965), MacQueen (1967), and McRae (1971).

Evaluation of Clusters

There has been considerable attention given to the "validation" of clustering solutions. Unfortunately, the task of ensuring that a specific clustering solution is "valid," or is the "correct" one, can sometimes be quite difficult. This topic has been treated in detail by Aldenderfer and Blashfield (1984). Thus we need not repeat their discussion, but need only to list the major approaches to validation, and provide some assessment of them.

Replication

One method of evaluating clustering solutions is the old standard of replication. One way to gain faith in your solution (both the number and composition of clusters) is to replicate it. This can be done by applying the same method to different samples or data sets, or even by dividing your single data set into two "equal" parts (the "split-half" method) to see if the same solution is obtained upon both halves. A somewhat different sort of "replication" is when different methods are used repeatedly on the same data set and results are compared. This is what we did in this chapter when we repeatedly analyzed Stephenson's (1953) Q-data of Table 3.3, and consistently retrieved the same clusters, regardless of the specific method used.

Significance Tests on External Variables

We can distinguish between "internal" variables (those used in the original cluster construction), and "external" variables (those not used in the original cluster construction). Aldenderfer and Blashfield (1984) consider use of external variables one of the best ways to validate a clustering solution, even though they note that it is infrequently used and can be difficult to use. This procedure consists of using significance tests to compare clusters on variables that were not used to create the original clusters. If the clusters are not significantly different on the new variables, then this is some evidence of their validity.

The problem with this approach is that it can be difficult and expensive to collect relevant criterion data. However, this procedure is worth applying when it is feasible. As Aldenderfer and Blashfield (1984, p. 67) say, "The value of a cluster solution that has successfully passed an external validation is much greater than a solution that has not."

Monte Carlo Procedures

Another validation procedure discussed by Aldenderfer and Blashfield (1984) that has some promise is a Monte Carlo procedure. Basically, this approach involves Monte Carlo procedures using random number generators to construct an artificial data set with the same general features of the original data set. The same clustering technique is then used on both the real and the artificial data, and the results are compared. For an extensive worked example, see Aldenderfer and Blashfield (1984, pp. 67-75).

Other Approaches

Other approaches to validation include cophenetic correlation, used only on hierarchical, agglomerative clustering methods, and significance tests on internal variables. Despite the popularity of both methods, Aldenderfer and Blashfield (1984, pp. 64-65) raise some real reservations about their use. For further discussion of these techniques, as well as additional references, please refer to Aldenderfer and Blashfield (1984).

The Interpretation of Clusters

The interpretation of clusters or taxa is perhaps a little more complex and multifaceted than the interpretation of conceptual types, as discussed in Chapter 2. To see what clusters represent, and how they can be interpreted, let us consider the clusters formed earlier in this chapter based on Stephenson's (1953) 121 introversion-extroversion (Jungian) items. Our analysis yielded one cluster composed of objects (individuals) A, B, C, D, E, F, G, and H; and a second cluster composed of objects I, J, K, L,

M, N, and O. In contrast to the type concepts discussed in Chapter 2, these two clusters are not concepts or constructs, but are empirical groupings, one containing eight individuals and one containing seven individuals. The individuals in each group comprise a polythetic class. For example, in Cluster 1, the eight individuals are the most similar on the basis of all 121 variables on which the Q-correlations are based.

What, exactly, can we tell about the eight individuals in Cluster 1? We know that they form a polythetic class, in all likelihood. While it is not strictly impossible for the cluster to be monothetic, this would require that all eight individuals have identical scores on all 121 variables. It seems rather evident from the intercorrelations that this is not the case. For example, the Q-correlation between B and E is only .242 (see Table 3.3). If B and E were identical on all 121 items their correlation would surely be much higher (if not 1.0). Thus we conclude that Cluster 1 is polythetic. But is it fully polythetic? This would mean that none of the 121 characteristics were possessed by all eight persons in the cluster. Is this true? Unfortunately, we really have no way to tell, short of going back to the original data (which Stephenson did not report) and examining the score of each of the eight individuals on each of the 121 variables (968 scores).

The fact that we cannot ascertain whether the cluster is fully polythetic merely from examination of the output of the cluster technique underscores the limitation of common clustering techniques for the interpretation of clusters. Most cluster output presents only clusters of objects (for Q-correlations) or clusters of variables (for R-correlations) but not both simultaneously. An exception to this rule is Hartigan's (1975) block clustering method, which simultaneously clusters objects and variables. Because we lack the simultaneous output showing the scores of individuals on variables, we cannot determine the degree of polytheticism. Further, we are limited in describing and naming the clusters. Still further, in most cases we will not attempt to construct a type concept for the empirically derived taxa.

For example, examining Cluster 1 and Cluster 2, what type concepts or constructs would you say they represent? Would you say that Cluster 1 represents introversion and Cluster 2 represents extroversion? This is what Stephenson (1953, p. 170) implies, but he can do so only on the basis of extra knowledge about the data set. From merely viewing the cluster output, we have no basis of drawing such conclusions, although we might subsequently be able to make such statements through further examination of each individual's scores on the 121 variables.

However, what if we had begun the analysis with R-correlations (correlations among the 121 variables) rather than Q-correlations (correlations among the 15 persons)? If we had R-clusters, we would have clusters of variables. In this case we might be able to place theoretical labels on the clusters through examination of the principal variables in each cluster. For example, we might determine that Cluster 1 was composed primarily of characteristics representing introversion, while Cluster 2 was composed primarily of extroversion variables. From the Q-data that we currently have available, however, we can make no such inferences.

Advantages and Disadvantages of Clustering

We have discussed the advantages and disadvantages of classification in general in some detail. In concluding this chapter it may be helpful to discuss some advantages and disadvantages specific to the quantitative clustering techniques discussed here. We are speaking here of generally automated, computerized statistical methods of cluster analysis.

Advantages

Sneath and Sokal (1973, p. 11) list six advantages of numerical taxonomy that are of interest to us here.

1. Numerical taxonomy aids in the integration of data.
2. Automation of numerical taxonomy leads to greater efficiency, enabling much taxonomic work to be done by machine with less highly trained workers.
3. The quantitatively coded data of numerical taxonomy can be integrated with existing electronic data processing systems.
4. Quantitative methods provide better classifications than nonquantitative, more subjective, conventional taxonomic methods. This is because the quantitative methods provide greater discrimination of taxonomic differences and are more sensitive in delimiting taxa.
5. The creation of explicit data tables for numerical taxonomy has led to use of more and better described characters (variables).
6. The development of numerical taxonomy has led to the reexamination of principles of taxonomy and the purposes of classification.

Disadvantages

Although Sneath and Sokal (1973) provided a comprehensive list of advantages for quantitative, computerized methods of creating empirical taxa, they did not list disadvantages specific to the approach. Obviously there are some disadvantages to a strictly quantitative empirical approach, and I will list them now.

1. The efficacy of the taxonomy is limited by the quality of the input data and its measurement. If the proper specimens cannot be found, if sampling is improper, or measurement is inadequate, then the taxonomy will suffer.

2. As we have seen, quantitative, empirically derived taxa can sometimes be difficult to interpret. If we have Q-clusters, we often know little about the specific variables on which the cluster is based. Similarly, if we have R-clusters, we know virtually nothing about the specific objects in each cluster. Rarely (as with Hartigan's 1975 method) does a method provide us with information about objects and variables simultaneously.

3. There may be problems of inference and generalization. While the taxa may suffice for the given data set from which they were constructed, we may not be sure of our ability to generalize these taxa to other samples or to the entire population.

4. Another problem with quantitative, empirically derived taxa is that they may be of limited theoretical and conceptual utility. It may be difficult to find the appropriate conceptual labels for them and to incorporate them into existing bodies of theory.

5. A disadvantage shared by other classification schemes and also by other statistical techniques, is the inherently static nature of quantitatively derived taxa. Although it is possible to make these methods dynamic (or at least partially so), this generally requires extra effort on the part of the researcher.

In addition to these five limitations, four other "cautions" are also listed by Aldenderfer and Blashfield (1984) and bear repeating here.

6. Clustering methods are often relatively simple procedures, and not supported by detailed statistical reasoning. They are best treated as simple "rules of thumb" rather than as the last word, or definitive solutions.

7. Clustering techniques are multidisciplinary, and may carry the biases of the particular discipline from which they are derived. This is clear enough in

the fact that many of the numerical taxonomic techniques have biological goals that may be somewhat different from the purposes of social scientists.

8. Although most researchers use cluster analysis to seek clusters, clustering techniques are generally structure imposing (rather than cluster seeking). That is, clustering techniques will generally impose structure (find clusters) regardless of the particular data used. To illustrate this point, we can construct a hypothetical data set, and if it contains similarity, clustering methods will impose clusters. These are not natural clusters, however; strictly speaking, they are not even artificial clusters—they are fictional clusters. This should not be taken to mean that clustering techniques cannot seek and find natural clusters, only that the techniques may impose clusters if the natural clusters are not there. As a case in point, Stephenson's (1953) data discussed earlier in this chapter contain two natural clusters that have been successfully sought and found (replicated) many times by many clustering techniques and by Q-factor analysis. Thus, there is no question that the techniques have found these natural clusters, rather than merely imposing clusters on the data.

9. A final problem is the lack of a unique clustering solution. As Aldenderfer and Blashfield (1984) note, different clustering techniques can yield different clusters from the same data set. This indicates lack of an underlying, unique, mathematical or statistical definition of a cluster. Some critics see this as a distinct limitation of clustering and would greatly prefer to see all techniques yield the same clusters.

In my opinion, however, this may be an exaggerated criticism. Different measures of association such as phi, Yule's Q, and so forth, will yield different values, as they are computed by different formulas. We accept this and choose among them for the one that best suits our needs. We do not criticize them for failing to provide a "unique" measure of association. We should also accept the fact that different clustering algorithms yield different results. Further, this will only be a practical problem in cases of intermediate similarity levels. If correlations are lacking in the data set, no clustering technique can manufacture homogeneous clusters, because the empirical homogeneity is just not there.

Conversely, if the data set exhibits a high degree of intercorrelation, almost all techniques will ultimately derive the same clusters, as was true in our examples using Stephenson's (1953) data earlier in this chapter. It is only where correlations are intermediate, and clustering solutions thus ambiguous, that some techniques will derive different (and perhaps better) clusters than others. Here, the key is to assess these clusters, to see which ones are the best. Methods of assessment of clusters include correlation techniques, significance tests, replications, and Monte Carlo procedures. For further discussion see Aldenderfer and Blashfield (1984, pp. 26-74).

4. RELATIONS AMONG TECHNIQUES

We have discussed conceptual typological methods (Chapter 2) and quantitative cluster analytic methods (Chapter 3) separately and in essentially chronological order in terms of their development. The conceptual techniques were developed first, before the advent of computerization, while clustering techniques have largely been developed since the 1950s. In order to derive full value from our study of classification techniques, it is crucial that we understand the relationships between these two developments as well as possible. After this discussion is concluded, we will relate these methods to other techniques such as factor analysis, multidimensional scaling, and multiple discriminant analysis.

Linking Types and Taxa

In retrospect, there are three major differences between types and taxa. Types generally are conceptual (rather than empirical), are monothetic, and are based on R-analysis. That is, although they are not statistically formed, the verbal procedure can be identified as R-analysis rather than Q-analysis, because it works with variables rather than objects or cases. In contrast, taxa formed through cluster analysis tend to be empirical, polythetic, and based on Q-analysis (although clusters can also be formed via R-analysis as well). Given these three chief differences, how can we best relate types and taxa?

This question can be answered from two directions—from types to taxa; or from taxa to types. Proceeding first from types to taxa, let us see how we can bridge the gap on all three fronts. The first task is to go from conceptual to empirical. This is rather straightforward and merely involves the identification of empirical cases for each conceptual cell. This has been discussed previously. The empirical cases found for each cell of the typology (such as Table 1.1) can be seen as equivalent to a taxon formed through cluster analysis. For example, if we identified 10 cases for cell 1 of Table 1.1, these would form an empirical group or cluster. This "cluster" is monothetic, however, and so would differ from the average cluster formed through cluster analysis, which is polythetic.

The second task in bridging the gap from types to taxa is to convert from monothetic to polythetic. This has already been discussed in some detail. As pointed out previously, we can merge cells of Table 1.1, for example, in various ways to form polythetic groups that are equivalent to the taxa formed through cluster analysis. The third task is to relate conceptual types based on *R*-analysis (analysis of variables) to taxa formed through *Q*-analysis. There are three basic approaches to this. One has just been suggested—to find objects (*Q*-analysis) that are examples of *R*-analysis types. This is a switch from *R* to *Q*. Another approach is to use *R*-analysis for clustering, which is simple enough. A third approach is to use *Q*-analysis for forming conceptual types. This is the least satisfactory, as it would provide a group of objects, but no information on the variable characteristics that account for their similarity.

Now consider the other direction—from taxa to types. Here the task entails going from empirical to conceptual; from polythetic to monothetic; and from *Q*-analysis to *R*-analysis. Going from empirical to conceptual entails formulating a concept, label, or name to represent the type. If the cluster is found via *R*-analysis, conceptualization is in terms of the primary variables. For example, in the illustrations presented in Chapter 3, we clustered objects (persons) A through H into Cluster 1 and I through O into Cluster 2. According to Stephenson (1953, pp. 168-170), Cluster 1 is composed of eight women and Cluster 2 of seven men. Further, Stephenson says that there is evidence for two main factors:

> The one for the women represents an introversion conception that each has about herself . . . and that for the men an extroversion conception that each man has about himself. (Stephenson, 1953, p. 170)

Thus, we can call Cluster 1 introversion and Cluster 2 extroversion. Notice, however, that such an inference cannot be made solely from knowing that Cluster 1, for example, includes persons A through H. Rather, knowledge of the 121 variables on which the clusters are based is required.

The second task involves a transition from polythetic to monothetic. Generally speaking, one cannot take a truly polythetic (especially a fully polythetic) cluster and transform it into a monothetic cluster. This is simply because full polytheticism indicates that there just is not sufficient similarity existent in the data to achieve monotheticism. Thus in many cases one is stuck with polythetic taxa and can never achieve monotheticism—the degree of imperfection in "the real world" simply does not allow it.

A researcher who insists on monothetic taxa can, however, seek them through cluster analysis if he or she is willing to make some compromises. The way to construct monothetic clusters is simply to discard all characters that vary within a group, as did Lockhart and Hartman (1963).

Another ploy adopted by Williams and Lambert (1959) is to use a divisive method that forms only two clusters and that clusters on only a single variable, choosing the variable that will best separate the two clusters.

The third task is to achieve *R*-analytic clusters through cluster analysis. This makes them compatible with the *R*-analytic types found through qualitative methods. This is achieved easily, by simply using *R*-correlations rather than *Q*-correlations in the cluster analysis.

Cluster Analysis and Factor Analysis

Now that we have compared types and taxa, it may be heuristic to compare clusters with factors. Fortunately, this comparison is rather easy and can be summarized in a few words. The chief difference between cluster analysis and factor analysis is that in the former, variance is not partitioned among clusters, while in the latter, variance is partitioned (divided) among factors. In other words, in *Q*-cluster analysis an object cannot be a member of two or more clusters simultaneously, but must be assigned wholly to the cluster it fits with the best. In contrast, in *Q*-factor analysis, an object may have a factor loading on all factors, as its variance is divided among them.

As an example, return to our analysis of Chapter 3, where we used Stephenson's (1953) data, as presented in our Table 3.3, to find two clusters, Cluster 1 (A, B, C, D, E, F, G, H) and Cluster 2 (I, J, K, L, M, N, O). Stephenson (1953, pp. 168-172) performed a *Q*-factor analysis on the same data, enabling a direct comparison of *Q*-cluster analysis and *Q*-factor analysis. He used a Thurstone centroid factor analysis and extracted two factors. He presented both the unrotated factors (I and II), and the same factors with a rotation of approximately 45° (I′ and II′) as shown in Table 4.1. Notice that each object has a loading on both factors I and II (Stephenson, 1953, p. 169, Table 6) in the factor analysis, where each object was a member of only a single cluster. In contrast, for example, object A (a woman) loads .46 on factor I and .38 on factor II (the unrotated factors), while object O (a man) loads .47 on factor I and −.46 on factor II.

Because variance is not partitioned in clustering, the two clusters are clearly divided and rotation is not used. In contrast, in factor analysis, factor separation and interpretation are often greatly aided by rotation. This is the case in Stephenson's factor analysis here, where a rotation of approximately 45° yields factors I′ and II′ (see Table 4.1). Here, the eight women (A through H) have high positive loadings on factor I′, with

TABLE 4.1
Factor Saturation for Table 3.3

	I	II	I'	II"
A	.46	.38	.60	.00
B	.48	.33	.58	.06
C	.57	.46	.73	.02
D	.63	.46	.78	.06
E	.56	.25	.59	.17
F	.52	.41	.66	.02
G	.37	.36	.52	-.04
H	.54	.43	.70	.02
I	.30	-.36	.00	.47
J	.49	-.44	.08	.65
K	.42	-.40	.07	.58
L	.32	-.44	-.04	.55
M	.37	-.44	.00	.58
N	.36	-.33	.06	.49
O	.47	-.46	.06	.66

SOURCE: Reprinted from W. Stephenson (1953) *The Study of Behavior* (p. 169). Chicago: University of Chicago Press. Used by permission of the publisher.
NOTE: n = 121 Jungian statements assessed for self-appraisal by 15 students; 8 women (A to H) and 7 men (I to O). I and II are centroid unrotated factors; I' and II" are the same rotated approximately 45°.

loadings near zero on factor II', while the seven men (I through O) have high positive loadings on factor II', with loadings near zero on factor I'. This high degree of factor separation enables us in effect to place A through H on factor I', and I through O on factor II', giving approximately the same results as the various cluster analyses that we presented in Chapter 3 for these data.

At first glance, the fact that factor analysis partitions the variance from a single variable or object among the various factors, while cluster analysis does not, might seem to be a distinct advantage for factor analysis, since it seems to be more accurate and efficient and yields more detail. In reality, however, many users of factor analysis often make it into a sort of de facto cluster analysis, by interpreting each variable or object on only a single factor (on which it loads the highest), and ignoring its loadings on the other less important factors. As an example of this, which factor pairs in Table 4.1 would you prefer to interpret, factors I and II, or factors I' and II'? They are the same except for the rotation. Factors I and II, however, show confusing loadings for the same person on each factor. It is easier and "neater" to interpret factors I' and II', which are in reality more like clusters, with each person loading significantly on only one factor and near zero on the other. Thus, although the factor analysis may yield more information, many times users in effect throw away this extra information and attempt to get their cases or variables to have principal loadings on only a single factor, thus in effect transforming them into a sort of de facto cluster analysis.

Although the partitioning of variance and the rotation of factors are the major differences between factor analysis and cluster analysis, there are some other differences between the two methods as well. One is that factor analysis generally requires continuous data, preferably interval or ratio data (although this assumption is often violated). A caveat for both cluster and factor analysis is to be sure that one has the proper data set. For R-analysis, this means preferably a large, random set of individuals, with a rather large number of variables. For example, an R-factor analysis or cluster analysis might have 75 variables measured on a sample of 1,000 persons. For R-analysis the rule of thumb is to have at least several times as many objects as variables.

For Q-analysis, the matrix is inverted and so are the requirements placed on the data set. Here, one should have several times as many variables as objects. Thus we might wish to have a sample of 100 persons, each measured on 400 variables. This requirement is often a hindrance for social scientists, who are not accustomed to measuring so many variables or to limiting their sample of objects. Another problem is that while we can generally identify a universe or population of objects in social science from which to choose a random sample of N objects, we generally cannot identify a universe or population of variables and thus have trouble securing the random sample of variables required for Q-analysis. Thus, social scientists will often attempt a Q-cluster analysis with a data set more appropriate for R-analysis (more objects than variables), which can lead to rather serious degree-of-freedom problems. This is because if one has a great many objects measured on a relatively few variables, some of the objects may by chance share values on a particular variable, thus exaggerating the real level of similarity.

If one has only a few objects measured on many variables as suggested for Q-analysis, it is much less likely that some objects would appear to be similar merely by chance, thus leading them to be clustered together inappropriately. The requirements of Q-analysis are often less onerous for biological numerical taxonomists who may have available only a few objects (particularly in the case of rare specimens), but who can easily measure a large number of characteristics for each specimen (especially if they use binary coding).

To summarize, in cluster analysis we in effect draw boundaries around clusters of objects in a property space. The boundaries are drawn so that each object is in one (but only one) group. Thus the clusters are mutually exclusive and exhaustive. In contrast, in factor analysis, we place a factor through a cluster of vectors. Each object is represented by a vector, and each factor represents a condensation of the vectors. An object's variance is divided between factors. Thus the set of factors is not mutually exclusive and exhaustive. For further discussion of factor analysis, see the volumes in this series by Kim and Mueller (1978a, 1978b).

Cluster Analysis and Multidimensional Scaling

One rather close neighbor of classification procedures is multidimensional scaling. The importance of this technique is underscored by the fact that at least four volumes in this series are devoted to it (see Arabie, Carroll, & DeSarbo, 1987; Jacoby, 1991; Kruskal & Wish, 1978; and Weller & Romney, 1990). Multidimensional scaling is rather complex and not always easily understood. Further, the field encompasses a sometimes confusing variety of techniques and approaches. However, a sample illustration will suffice to show the basic relationship between cluster analysis and multidimensional scaling.

Examine the property space of Figure 4.1. This figure shows the three-dimensional representation of Q-analysis (Figure 4.1a) and R-analysis (Figure 4.1b). In the representation of Q-analysis the dimensions of the property space are variables and the points in space represent the objects to be clustered. In R-analysis, the dimensions of the property space are objects and the points in space represent the variables to be clustered.

Focusing on Figure 4.1a, notice that the task of cluster analysis is to delimit the clusters in the property space. We cannot move the points around in space, but we can move the boundaries of the clusters. Because the six objects fall naturally into two separated groups of three each, it is relatively easy to delimit two clusters. The two clusters are situated in a property space comprised of three dimensions, the most that we can easily represent on two-dimensional paper.

Remember, however, we just said that for Q-cluster analysis, one ideally should have a data set with several times as many variables as

72

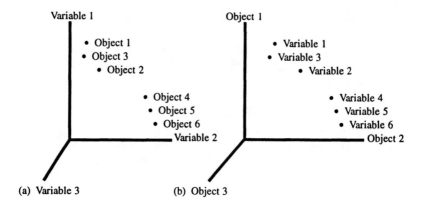

Figure 4.1. (a) Three-dimensional representation of objects as points in a space where variables are dimensions. (b) Variables as points in a space where objects are dimensions.
SOURCE: Bailey (1974). Reprinted by permission from Jossey-Bass, Inc.

objects. Thus, to cluster six objects, three dimensions are not sufficient. We should have at least 20 or so variables (dimensions).

To illustrate a proper Q-analysis, recall our analysis of Stephenson's (1953) Q-data (Table 3.3). Stephenson had data on 121 variables for 15 persons. We would prefer to begin the cluster analysis by drawing a picture showing the location of all 15 persons in the property space of 121 dimensions. If we could do this, then perhaps we could simply perform the cluster analysis by drawing boundaries around groups of points. It is impossible, however, to represent all 121 dimensions on paper simultaneously (although we could represent them two at a time).

One function of multidimensional scaling is to scale some of the 121 variables so that the number of dimensions is reduced from 121 to some smaller number, perhaps even 2 or 3. This is in effect an R-analysis (while clustering the objects remains a Q-analysis). Multidimensional scaling (MDS) usually begins with a set of objects. Objects can be very broadly defined. As Arabie et al. (1987, p. 7) say, "By 'object,' we mean stimuli, political candidates, biological entities, variables, or whatever other objects the user seeks to position in a spatial representation." For example, in the first application of MDS by Kruskal and Wish (1978, pp. 7-9), the "objects" were cities. The basic data for MDS is a matrix containing data on similarity or dissimilarity between all pairs of the set of objects. The goal is to achieve the best fit property space for representing the objects as points in a visual, spatial representation. Generally, the fewer dimensions used, the worse the fit. The goal is to find a low-dimensional solution (perhaps two or three dimensions) that provides visual representation, while also providing an adequate representation of the points in the space.

After the visual representation is achieved (e.g., yielding a property space similar to those in Figure 4.1), the researcher can visually examine the points in space (objects) to see if any clustering is evident. Sometimes it may be possible to draw boundaries around sets of points, yielding adequate clusters. Arabie et al. (1987, p. 54), however, argue strongly against such visual subjective clustering. They stress that MDS and clustering are complementary. Rather than cluster visually in the reduced space, they highly recommend using some clustering algorithms, such as the ones we discussed in Chapter 3. They say:

It is our strong recommendation that MDS analyses be accompanied by cluster analyses and vice versa whenever the data permit. Furthermore, there is a corollary to this recommendation: performing a legitimate cluster analysis requires using a method that explicitly and objectively seeks clusters (one should *not* try visually to "define" clusters on the basis of a spatial representation of the objects resulting from an analysis based on such continuous models as principal components analysis, factor analysis or spatial MDS). It is of course natural to refer to groupings and other spatial patterns in such a configuration of objects, but to elevate such subjective groupings to the status of "clusters" and suggest that they have reality other than visual is misleading. (Arabie et al., 1987, p. 54. Italics in the original.)

Cluster Analysis and
Multiple Discriminant Analysis

Another close neighbor to clustering is multiple discriminant analysis. Consult Klecka (1980) for an introduction to this method. A person with only passing familiarity with clustering and discriminant procedures might, at first glance, think that they were basically the same, as both seem to cluster objects into groups. There is, however, a very basic difference between the two: discriminant analysis begins with (and requires) pre-existing groups, while cluster analysis seeks to form its own groups.

As we noted in Chapter 3, a fundamental dilemma in cluster analysis is that it tries to delimit clusters so as to minimize within-group variance, but has no way to measure this variance until the group is delimited. Thus the dilemma: If we could properly measure the within-group variance, then we could properly delimit the group; but on the other hand, if we could properly delimit the group, then we could properly measure the within-group variance. This is sort of the reverse of the "chicken-or-the-egg" problem, because in this case, neither the chicken nor the egg come first.

Happily, discriminant analysis is able to bypass this dilemma by beginning with groups (clusters) that already exist prior to the use of the discriminant analysis. Although this greatly facilitates execution of the model, it is also quite restrictive, meaning that we cannot use discriminant analysis as a clustering technique (for forming clusters), but can only use it in cases where we have a preexisting classification.

As with multidimensional scaling, clustering and multiple discriminant analysis are complementary techniques and make good partners when used in conjunction with each other. In this symbiotic relationship, cluster analysis is used first, and multiple discriminant analysis is used second. Cluster analysis forms the clusters, or provides a preexisting classification for multiple discriminant analysis. In this case, we need not insist on cluster analysis or even a quantitative technique, but can use any classification technique, including qualitative methods of typology construction, as discussed in Chapter 2. If we construct a verbal typology, however, we must then have some method of assigning cases to cells, for it is necessary for empirical cases to be assigned to groups. Thus the only requirement for multiple discriminant analysis is that we start with a preexisting classification (and, of course, have an adequate data set). The point is that it does not matter how the preexisting empirical groupings were formed.

After cases are assigned to groups, multiple discriminant analysis can then be used. Discriminant analysis uses the variables linearly to predict the group in which the individual belongs. That is, the data for multiple discriminant analysis are a set of empirical cases (objects) assigned to groups, and a set of continuously measured variables (preferably interval or ratio) measured for each case. As an example, recall our clustering of Stephenson's (1953) data into Cluster 1 (introversion) and Cluster 2 (extroversion). Cluster 1 contained eight women (A through H), and Cluster 2 contained seven men (I through O). Suppose now that we obtain a new sample of 10 additional persons, surveyed on the same 121 Jungian statements. The problem is to determine (on the basis of the variables) which cluster they should be assigned to.

Multiple discriminant analysis is perfect for this task. It uses the 121 statements to predict a score for each person on a dimension that is the best linear combination of the scores. The first discriminant function accounts for the most variance. Later discriminant functions, if any, are orthogonal to the earlier ones. By determining the group mean for each cluster, discriminant analysis can enable us to determine whether an individual's score is closer to the mean of Cluster 1 or Cluster 2 on the discriminant function, thus allowing us to identify the correct cluster for each new individual. Thus clustering and discriminant analysis form a symbiotic partnership. Clustering forms the initial classification, and multiple discriminant analysis is subsequently used for identifying the group to which additional cases should be assigned.

Classification and Systems Analysis

Another approach that has clear links to classification is systems analysis (see Bailey, 1982, 1985, 1990, 1994). Systems analysts view systems as interrelated sets of components that have a boundary and are often hierarchical in nature. This sounds remarkably like the definition of a cluster. Some points of comparison between systems and classifications may be listed briefly.

1. Natural Versus Artificial. Both systems analysts and classification analysts are primarily interested in the study of naturally occurring, rather than artificial, groups.
2. Conceptual Versus Empirical. Both systems analysts and classification analysts study at both the conceptual and the empirical levels.
3. Overlapping Groups. Both classification analysts and systems analysts focus primarily on nonoverlapping groups. Both approaches, however, have recognized the existence of "fuzzy sets," and this notion has been applied to both "fuzzy clusters" (Zadeh, 1977) and "fuzzy systems" (Zadeh, 1979).
4. Single Level Versus Hierarchical. This is another point of similarity, as the concept of hierarchy is used in both systems analysis and classification analysis. In both approaches, probably the majority of cases studied are hierarchical, although nonhierarchical cases are also recognized and studied.
5. Boundaries. Both fields must delimit their entities (classes, clusters, or systems), and both use the notion of boundary for this purpose.

6. Synchronic Versus Diachronic Analysis. Both classes and systems can either be diachronic or synchronic; however, both fields have been criticized for focusing on predominantly static models.

These six points do not exhaust the linkages between systems and classes, but do provide discussion of the chief factors. For further discussion of the similarity between classifications and systems, including these six points and others, please see Bailey (1982, 1985).

After discussing the links between classification techniques and other approaches, our conclusion here is that the obvious strengths of various classification procedures should not be used in a vacuum, but can be made even greater by properly using the classification techniques in conjunction with other research procedures. Very rarely will a classification technique interfere with the operation of one of the other methods or contradict its results. Generally, the results are complementary when the two techniques are used in conjunction with one another.

For example if we wish to run a *Q*-cluster analysis, we need not use it in isolation, but can supplement it in various ways. To begin with, we might use the variables to form a qualitative, conceptual typology, whose monothetic cells could be used for the heuristic evaluation of the clusters, which can be viewed as polythetic reductions of the full typology. After this is done, it might be useful to compare the clusters with the results of a *Q*-factor analysis, as we did above for Stephenson's (1953) data. Finally, discriminant analysis could be used if we wished to identify additional cases for the clusters.

As another example, if we constructed a multidimensional scale, we might turn to cluster analysis for interpretation of the points in the final space. All in all, it is clear that classification techniques in social science not only remain valuable in the classical qualitative sense, but are quantitatively important as well and blend well with other facets of research.

5. SUMMARY AND CONCLUSIONS

This monograph has shown, in chronological order, the substantial array of fundamental classificatory tools now at the disposal of social scientists. The resourceful researcher should be able to apply these tools efficaciously—from full conceptual typologies, to reduced typologies achieved through the various reduction techniques, to construction of polythetic empirical taxonomies through cluster analysis. The idea is to be aware of the full range of classificatory techniques at your disposal and to use them in ways that complement each other and integrate your efforts, rather than in ways that contradict or fragment. Although it is common in social science for a researcher to adopt either a qualitative or a quantitative perspective and virtually exclude the alternative approach, our discussion here has shown that, at least when it comes to classificatory techniques, the qualitative and quantitative approaches are not contradictory by any means, but rather are complementary and symbiotic.

Because the qualitative conceptual typological approach predates computerization, we might infer that computerized methods of numerical taxonomy have supplanted the qualitative approaches or rendered them obsolete. In fact, we have seen that this is not so. If anything, the computerized methods may have revitalized the conceptual techniques and given them new life by removing some of the pressure for them to deal with empirical data. The Q-analytic methods favored by numerical taxonomists duly complement the R-typological methods of verbal theorists, but in no way replace them.

Classification Resources

Unfortunately, there is no extant resource of tools for aiding social scientists in the construction of conceptual typologies, or ideal or polar types. The reader must rely primarily on published resources, such as Chapters 1 and 2 of this volume, and the references provided there.

Happily, there are more adequate resources for cluster analysis. Although the number of available clustering programs is not as large and perhaps as adequate as the programs for some other statistical procedures, nevertheless they are available. These programs have been well described by Aldenderfer and Blashfield (1984, pp. 74-80), and the reader is referred there for details. I need only mention some of the chief programs and update them somewhat.

One of the major clustering software packages is CLUSTAN (Wishart, 1987). CLUSTAN contains eight SAHN programs (hierarchical agglomerative methods) as discussed in Chapter 3, as well as other programs. Another program of interest to social scientists is BCTRY (Tryon & Bailey, 1970), based on Tryon's pioneering methods in psychology. Also of interest is NT-SYS (Rohlf, Kishpaugh, & Kirk, 1974), which is based on the biological approaches of numerical taxonomy as discussed in Sneath and Sokal (1973).

In addition to these packages devoted entirely to clustering, most of the standard statistical packages for the social sciences now have at least one clustering program (although that was not always true in the beginning). One of the best packages is BMDP (Dixon, 1983), which has procedures for single, complete, and average linkage agglomerative clustering. SAS (SAS Institute, 1982) contains centroid, Ward's, and average linkage hierarchical agglomerative methods. Euclidian distance, however, is the only measure available. SPSS (SPSS, 1988) currently has a cluster package available, although it previously did not. For further discussion see Aldenderfer and Blashfield (1984, pp. 74-80).

Classification Applications

We have presented a number of applications ranging from conceptual typologies to cluster analyses throughout this volume. It may be helpful, in concluding, to present additional examples from the literature. Referring to Figure 2.2 of Chapter 2, you will recall that we discussed three forms of classification: strictly conceptual typologies (X—Figure 2.2a); strictly empirical typologies (X'—Figure 2.2b); and combined conceptual/empirical, or indicator-level classification (X"—Figure 2.2c). Variations of all of these can be found in the literature.

Conceptual Typologies

Perusal of the social science literature shows examples of purely conceptual or (X) level qualitative typologies, as in Figure 2.2a. As one example, Wright and Cho (1992, p. 89) presented a "typology of class structure." They used three dimensions: the *property* dimension, the *authority* dimension, and the *expertise* dimension. They combined these dimensions to form a "basic class structure typology" that is divided into two parts, a six-celled typology for owners, and a nine-celled typology for employees. These are used in their analysis of friendship patterns across class boundaries. For further discussion please see Wright and Cho (1992).

In another study, Lie (1992, pp. 510-511) presents two typologies, one a "descriptive" typology of modes of exchange and the other an "explanatory" typology of modes of exchange. The descriptive typology is based on two dimensions: "region" (intraregional and interregional) and "social relations of exchange" (open trade and closed trade). When combined, these yield four cells: (1) market, (2) manorial, (3) entrepreneurial, and (4) mercantile. The explanatory typology is similar, yielding the same four cells but using different dimensions ("national centralization" and "local stratification"). For further discussion see Lie (1992).

Ethnographic Classification

In addition to conceptual typologies (X) as in Figure 2.2a, another form of qualitative classification is common in the social science literature. This is the combined conceptual/empirical taxonomy (X″) of Figure 2.2c. Widely used by ethnographers, these taxonomies begin with empirical data (X′). Observation of these data is then used as a basis for the formulation of names or labels (concepts) for the various taxa (X), leading to the indicator level (X″) classification of Figure 2.2c.

Qualitative classifications are widely used in qualitatively oriented research paradigms such as field research (ethnography). Ethnographers often do not have a quantitative orientation. They often do not begin research with specific hypotheses, preferring to let hypotheses, if any, develop during the observation of empirical data via the method of "grounded theory" (Glaser & Strauss, 1967). They also eschew reliance on statistical data analysis. Their data are often in the form of field notes. Some mechanism is needed for transforming these lengthy resource notes so that data, interpretations, and conclusions may be presented to readers. Typologies are admirably suited to this task.

Spradley and McCurdy (1972) refer to their classifications as taxonomies rather than typologies and emphasize the role of taxonomy in ethnography. They say that taxonomies are useful in the representation of cultural categories. They note that such cultural categories (types) can originate either from the researcher or from the subjects in the culture (or subculture) being studied. They give the example of homeless people. They say that these people are classified in various ways, such as: bums, vagrants, drunks, homeless men, or alcoholics (Spradley & McCurdy, 1972, p. 63). Spradley (1970), however, in studying homeless people, discovered that the major term that these people used for their own self-identification was "tramp." Further, there are enough different types of tramps to form a rather large typology: boxcar tramp, bindle stiff, working stiff, and so forth. Still further, some of these types of tramps can be again divided into subtypes. For example, "working stiffs" can be variously identified by the type of work they do, such as: harvest tramp, tramp miner, fruit tramp, construction tramp, or sea tramp (see Spradley & McCurdy, 1972, p. 65).

Many other taxonomies are presented by Spradley and McCurdy. As their book illustrates, taxonomy is a major tool for the presentation of ethnographic data.

Cluster Analysis

The cluster analytic methods of numerical taxonomy have been applied to the study of organizational analysis by McKelvey (1982). We noted earlier that a difficult problem for any analysis, whether it is theoretical, statistical, or classificatory, is the selection of a proper set of analytic variables. Often there is no set procedure for generating such variables, other than an adequate theory and prior research experience. Classification researchers interested in organizational analysis have long been concerned with discovering the "right" set of characteristics for the classification of organizations. Some of these efforts are described by McKelvey (1982, pp. 353-373). It may be helpful to discuss them here briefly and then refer the reader to McKelvey for further discussion.

Most researchers have divided organization characteristics into classes roughly dealing with characteristics of the organization's members, characteristics of the organization itself, and characteristics of the organization's environment. However, the specific classifications vary quite widely. The Sells categorization (McKelvey, 1982, pp. 354-358) includes personnel characteristics (such as aptitudes and skills, motivations, personality, age); organizational characteristics (such as procedures permitted, facilities, control of group members, rewards, autonomy); and environmental characteristics (such as climate, terrain, relation to other organizations).

The Warriner categories (McKelvey, 1982, pp. 360-364; Warriner, 1979) concentrate on four different views of organizations: as technical systems, social systems, power systems, or cultural systems—with all of these dimensions to be included in any list of organizational characteristics. Each of these four categories has a host of characteristics within it. For example, characteristics of the social system include structural characteristics (number and kinds of positions), criteria for allocation of persons to positions, patterns of relationships, and division of labor

(McKelvey, 1982, p. 361). In addition, McKelvey (1982, p. 365) presents his own categorization of taxonomic characters, which includes morphological characters, physiological characters, and geographical characters. McKelvey (1982) also has extensive discussion of all phases of the application of numerical taxonomy to the classification of organizations, including the discussion of specific clustering methods. Please see his book for further discussion.

Some good examples of cross-cultural clustering applications are found in the monograph by Ferligoj and Kramberger (1993, pp. 149-183), including a whole section on cluster applications, most of them in Slovenia (formerly a part of Yugoslavia). One study (Kropivnik et al., 1993) uses a hierarchical agglomerative clustering method to derive "typologies of variables" for the United States, Japan, and Slovenia. In another study, Hafner-Fink (1993) used Ward's method (discussed in Chapter 3) to generate a dendogram (also discussed in Chapter 3) of Slovene communes. The results indicate, among other things, a clustering of lower fertility in urban areas.

Turning to American social science, we also see a number of cluster analyses represented in the journals. For example, Vanneman (1977) wanted to study the occupational composition of American classes and found cluster analysis to be ideally suited to this task. Vanneman (1977) used the complete linkage hierarchical clustering method of Johnson (1967; see also Bailey, 1974). Applying this method to data from Detroit, Vanneman constructed a dendogram that contained five main clusters, each with subclusters. These five clusters are: (1) skilled, (2) semi-skilled (blue collar), (3) lower middle, (4) petty bourgeois, and (5) upper middle (white collar). Vanneman is critical of agglomerative clustering for the analysis of higher order clustering and prefers to apply divisive methods for this purpose, using gamma as a measure of association. Vanneman also presents considerable analysis and evaluation of cluster analysis, in addition to his research results. For further discussion, see Vanneman (1977).

In two more recent studies, both Ennis (1992) and Cappell and Guterbock (1992) modeled the myriad specialties within sociology. Because the specialties are so diverse, it is difficult to classify them and to find any underlying structure for them. In both studies, cluster analysis again proved ideal for this task and became the method of choice. Ennis (1992) used data from 13,265 members of the American Sociological Association (ASA) and used the specialty categories employed in the ASA 1990 Membership Directory. Ninety-six percent of the members listed at least one specialty area of interest, with 82% naming four areas of interest. Ennis used 53 specialty areas coded 1 if mentioned by a member and 0 if not. He used SPSS to conduct the cluster analysis, using an agglomerative average linkage method (for details see Ennis, 1992, p. 260). Ennis's analysis yields seven chief clusters, plus three unclustered specialties that he terms "isolates" (we would call them outliers). The three outliers are military sociology, biosociology, and the sociology of sport. The seven clusters are: (1) deviance, (2) demography and ecology, (3) politics and macrosociology, (4) theory and culture, (5) quantitative methods and mathematical sociology, (6) social psychology/medical/gender/family, and (7) stratification and work. All of these seven clusters contain additional specialties not mentioned here, but that stand out plainly as subclusters in Ennis's (1992, p. 261) dendogram.

Cappell and Guterbock (1992) also clustered sociological specialties. Rather than use a clustering algorithm directly, however, as Ennis (1992) did, they first used a maximum-likelihood metric, multidimensional scaling procedure, saying that: "Once a desired configuration of points is obtained, the estimated coordinates are used to cluster and plot the specialties" (Cappell & Guterbock, 1992, p. 269). The result is also a dendogram showing seven clusters (Cappell & Guterbock, 1992, p. 269), but without as many subclusters as Ennis's (1992, p. 261) results. They also determined that three basic dimensions underline these seven clusters: (1) microsociology/macrosociology, (2) critical/applied, and (3) professional power. These seven clusters (my names) are: (1) theory; (2) ecology, demography, and environment; (3) criminology, methodology, social psychology; (4) gender and family; (5) applied and medical sociology; (6) organizations and occupations; and (7) education and race/ethnicity. Again, the clusters contain other specializations in addition to the ones named here. Rather than try to list them all, I will simply refer the reader to the source (Cappell & Guterbock, 1992) for further information.

The last example I will provide is by Hogan, Eggebeen, and Clogg (1993). They use latent class analysis (see Bailey, 1974) to derive a categorical latent variable for their study of intergeneration exchanges. They say (Hogan et al., 1993, p. 1438) that: "The latent class model is often portrayed as a method of characterizing ideal-types, which are categorical by nature." Based on a number of variables describing exchanges among generations, such as "give assistance," "give advice," "receive advice," and "give money," the authors derive five latent classes (types of exchangers): low exchangers, (advice) givers, high exchangers, receivers, and co-residers (Hogan et al., 1993, p. 1443). Note that the examples presented here are not exhaustive of the types or number of applications in the social science literature, but merely illustrate some representative usages. I will now leave the discussion of examples and conclude the volume.

Concluding Remarks

To summarize, I would recommend that a researcher wishing to avail himself or herself of the best classification techniques in social science be familiar with the following. First, the researcher should be familiar with the advantages and limitations of classificatory typological methods, including full typologies, the conceptual nature of types, the relationship of typologies to theories, the derivation of typologies from theory through deduction, ideal types, constructed types, the logic of classes, polar types, substruction, and reduction. The nature of monotheticism should also be familiar. Next, the researcher should be familiar with the goals and limitations of clustering methods, including the empirical nature of taxa, the notion of polytheticism, basic agglomerative and divisive methods of clustering, the relation of taxa to types, and the identification of additional cases through multiple discriminant analysis.

If all of these concepts and techniques are mastered, the researcher should be able to derive optimum benefit from the extant classificatory techniques currently available for social scientists. I urge you to use these fundamental and valuable methods to their fullest. If you do so, I think that you will find that they form a firm foundation for both your theoretical and research (including statistical) endeavors. They will greatly complement and enrich the whole process of social theorizing and research. Your applications of classification to a wide variety of social science areas are needed and welcomed.

The fact that classification is ubiquitous in our everyday life does not mean that it can be taken for granted or that classification efforts cannot be improved. In fact, because classification is so ubiquitous, it is relatively easy to overlook it. I thus wish to close with a strong plea for researchers to help end the common neglect of classification efforts by never taking classification for granted, and by always striving diligently to improve the construction and use of our typologies and taxonomies.

REFERENCES

ALDENDERFER, M. E., and BLASHFIELD, R. K. (1984) *Cluster Analysis*. Sage University Paper series on Quantitative Applications in the Social Sciences, 07-044. Beverly Hills, CA: Sage.

ANDERBERG, M. R. (1973) *Cluster Analysis for Applications*. New York: Academic Press.

ARABIE, P., CARROLL, J. D., and DeSARBO, W. S. (1987) *Three-Way Scaling and Clustering*. Sage University Paper series on Quantitative Applications in the Social Sciences, 07-065. Newbury Park, CA: Sage.

BAILEY, K. D. (1972) "Polythetic reduction of monothetic property space," in H. L. Costner (ed.), *Sociological Methodology 1972*. San Francisco: Jossey-Bass.

BAILEY, K. D. (1973) "Monothetic and polythetic typologies and their relation to conceptualization measurement, and scaling." *American Sociological Review* 38: 18-32.

BAILEY, K. D. (1974) "Cluster analysis," in D. R. Heise (ed.), *Sociological Methodology 1975*, pp. 59-127. San Francisco: Jossey-Bass.

BAILEY, K. D. (1982) "Clusters as systems." *The Classification Society Bulletin* 5: 18-35.

BAILEY, K. D. (1983) "Sociological classification and cluster analysis." *Quality and Quantity* 17: 251-268.

BAILEY, K. D. (1984) "A three level measurement model." *Quality and Quantity* 18: 225-245.

BAILEY, K. D. (1985) "Systems as clusters." *Behavioral Science* 30: 98-107.

BAILEY, K. D. (1986) "Philosophical foundations of sociological measurement: A note on the three level model." *Quality and Quantity* 20: 327-337.

BAILEY, K. D. (1989) "Taxonomy and disaster: Prospects and problems." *International Journal of Mass Emergencies and Disasters* 7: 419-431.

BAILEY, K. D. (1990) *Social Entropy Theory*. Albany: SUNY Press.

BAILEY, K. D. (1992) "Typologies," in E. F. Borgatta and M. L. Borgatta (eds.), *Encyclopedia of Sociology*, pp. 2188-2194. New York: Macmillan.

BAILEY, K. D. (1993) "Strategies of nucleus formation in agglomerative clustering techniques." *Bulletin de Methodologie Sociologique* no. 38: 38-51.

BAILEY, K. D. (1994) *Sociology and the New Systems Theory: Toward a Theoretical Synthesis*. Albany: SUNY Press.

BALL, G. H. (1965) "Data analysis in the social sciences: What about the details?" in *American Federation of Information Processing Societies Conference Proceedings, Fall Joint Computer Conference*, Vol. 27, part 1, pp. 533-560. Washington, DC: Spartan Books.

BARTON, A. H. (1955) "The concept of property-space in social research," in P. F. Lazarsfeld and M. Rosenberg (eds.), *Language of Social Research*, pp. 40-53. Glencoe, IL: Free Press.

BECKER, H. (1940) "Constructive typology in the social sciences," in H. E. Barnes, H. Becker, and F. B. Becker (eds.), *Contemporary Social Theory*. New York: D. Appleton Century.

BECKER, H. (1950) *Through Values to Social Interpretation*. Durham, NC: Duke University Press.

BECKER, H. (1951) "Propaganda and the impotent German intellectual." *Social Forces* 29: 273-276.

BECKNER, M. (1959) *The Biological Way of Thought.* New York: Columbia University Press.

CAPECCHI, V. (1966) "Typologies in relation to mathematical models." *Ikon* suppl. no. 58: 1-62.

CAPPELL, C. L., and GUTERBOCK, T. M. (1992) "Visible colleges: The social and conceptual structure of sociology specialties." *American Sociological Review* 57: 266-273.

DIXON, W. (1983) *BMDP Statistical Software.* Berkeley: University of California Press.

DRIVER, H. E., and KROEBER, A. L. (1932) "Quantitative expression of cultural relationships." *University of California Publications in American Archeology and Ethnology* 31: 211-256.

DURKHEIM, E. (1893) *The Division of Labor in Society.* Translated by G. Simpson. Glencoe, IL: Free Press.

EDWARDS, A. W. F., and CAVALLI-SFORZA, L. L. (1965) "A method for cluster analysis." *Biometrics* 21: 362-375.

ENNIS, J. G. (1992) "The social organization of sociological knowledge: Modeling the intersection of specialties." *American Sociological Review* 57: 259-265.

EVERITT, B. S. (1980) *Cluster Analysis.* 2nd edition. London: Heinemann.

FERLIGOJ, A., and KRAMBERGER, A. (eds.) (1993) *Developments in Statistics and Methodology.* Ljubljana, Slovenia: University of Ljubljana, Faculty of Social Science.

FLEISS, J. L., and ZUBIN, J. (1969) "On the methods and theory of clustering." *Multivariate Behavioral Science* 4: 235-250.

FORGY, E. W. (1965, June) "Cluster analysis of multivariate data: Efficiency vs. interpretability of classifications." Paper presented at the WNAR Meeting, University of California, Riverside.

FRIEDMAN, H. P., and RUBIN, J. (1967) "On some invariant criteria for grouping data." *Journal of the American Statistical Association* 62: 1159-1178.

FRUCHTER, B. (1954) *Introduction to Factor Analysis.* Princeton, NJ: Van Nostrand.

GLASER, B. G., and STRAUSS, A. L. (1967) *The Discovery of Grounded Theory: Strategies for Qualitative Research.* Chicago: Aldine.

GOWER, J. C. (1967) "A comparison of some methods of cluster analysis." *Biometrics* 23: 623-637.

HAFNER-FINK, M. (1993) "Clustering methods in the context of comparative analysis—Ideological consciousness of classes in the former Yugoslavia," in A. Ferligoj and A. Kramberger (eds.), *Developments in Statistics and Methodology,* pp. 165-174. Ljubljana, Slovenia: University of Ljubljana, Faculty of Social Science.

HARTIGAN, J. A. (1975) *Clustering Algorithms.* New York: John Wiley.

HEMPEL, C. G. (1952) "Typological methods in the natural and social sciences." *Proceedings, American Philosophical Society, Eastern Division* 1: 656-686.

HOGAN, D. P., EGGEBEEN, D. J., and CLOGG, C. C. (1993) "The structure of intergenerational exchanges in American families." *American Journal of Sociology* 98: 1428-1458.

HOLZINGER, K. J. (1937) *Student Manual of Factor Analysis.* Chicago: University of Chicago, Department of Education.

HUDSON, H. E., and Associates. (eds.) (1982) *Classifying Social Data.* San Francisco: Jossey-Bass.

86

JACOBY, W. G. (1991) *Data Theory and Dimensional Analysis.* Sage University Paper series on Quantitative Applications in the Social Sciences, 07-078. Newbury Park, CA: Sage.

JARDINE, N., and SIBSON, R. (1968) "The construction of hierarchic and non-hierarchic classifications." *Computer Journal* 11: 177-184.

JARDINE, N., and SIBSON, R. (1971) *Mathematical Taxonomy.* London: John Wiley.

JOHNSON, S. C. (1967) "Hierarchical clustering schemes." *Psychometrika* 32: 154-241.

KIM, J. O., and MUELLER, C. W. (1978a) *Introduction to Factor Analysis.* Sage University Paper series on Quantitative Applications in the Social Sciences, 07-013. Beverly Hills, CA: Sage.

KIM, J. O., and MUELLER, C. W. (1978b) *Factor Analysis: Statistical Methods and Practical Issues.* Sage University Paper series on Quantitative Applications in the Social Sciences, 07-014. Beverly Hills, CA: Sage.

KLECKA, W. (1980) *Discriminant Analysis.* Sage University Paper series on Quantitative Applications in the Social Sciences, 07-019. Beverly Hills, CA: Sage.

KREPS, G. A. (ed.) (1989) "The boundaries of disaster research: Taxonomy and comparative research" (Special Issue). *International Journal of Mass Emergencies and Disasters* 7: 213-431.

KROPIVNIK, S., BELAK, E., BRESAR, A., CEBOKLI, M., GNIDOVEC, M., GRAHEK, J., HOCEVAR, R., KANDUC, A., KOGOVSEK, T., LOKENC, M., MACRU, M., MEDVESEK, M., POCAJT, J., SAKIC, D., ZORKO, A., and ZUPANCIC, M. (1993) "Comparative studies methodology—Clustering approaches: The case of motivation items in the USA, Japan, and Slovenia," in A. Ferligoj and A. Kramberger (eds.), *Developments in Statistics and Methodology,* pp. 149-163. Ljubljana, Slovenia: University of Ljubljana, Faculty of Social Science.

KRUSKAL, J. B., and WISH, M. (1978) *Multidimensional Scaling.* Sage University Paper series on Quantitative Applications in the Social Sciences, 07-011. Beverly Hills, CA: Sage.

LANCE, G. N., and WILLIAMS, W. T. (1967) "A general theory of classificatory sorting strategies: I: Hierarchical systems." *Computer Journal* 9: 373-380.

LAZARSFELD, P. F. (1937) "Some remarks on the typological procedures in social research." *Zeitschrift für Sozialforschung* 6: 119-139.

LIE, J. (1992) "The concept of modes of exchange." *American Sociological Review* 57: 508-523.

LOCKHART, W. R., and HARTMAN, P. A. (1963) "Formation of monothetic groups in quantitative bacterial taxonomy." *Journal of Bacteriology* 85: 68-77.

LORR, M. (1983) *Cluster Analysis for Social Scientists.* San Francisco: Jossey-Bass.

MacQUEEN, J. (1967) "Some methods for classification and analysis of multivariate observation," in L. M. LeCam and J. Neyman (eds.), *Proceedings of the Fifth Berkeley Symposium on Mathematical Statistics and Probability,* Vol. I, pp. 281-297. Berkeley: University of California Press.

MARTINDALE, D. (1959) "Sociological theory and the ideal type," in L. Gross (ed.), *Symposium on Sociological Theory,* pp. 57-91. New York: Harper & Row.

MARTINDALE, D. (1960) *The Nature and Types of Sociological Theory.* Boston: Houghton Mifflin.

MAYER, L. S. (1971) "A theory of cluster analysis when there exist multiple indicators of a theoretic concept." *Biometrics* 27: 143-155.

McKELVEY, B. (1982) *Organizational Systematics: Taxonomy, Evolution, Classification.* Berkeley: University of California Press.

McKINNEY, J. C. (1954) "Constructive typology in social research," in J. T. Doby, E. A. Suchman, J. C. McKinney, R. G. Francis, and J. P. Dean (eds.), *An Introduction to Social Research,* pp. 139-198. Harrisburg, PA: Stackpole.

McKINNEY, J. C. (1966) *Constructive Typology and Social Theory.* New York: Appleton-Century-Crofts.

McQUITTY, L. L. (1956) "Agreement analysis: Classifying persons by predominant patterns of responses." *British Journal of Statistical Psychology* 9: 5-16.

McQUITTY, L. L. (1957) "Elementary linkage analysis for isolating orthogonal and oblique types and typal relevancies." *Educational and Psychological Measurement* 17: 207-229.

McQUITTY, L. L. (1960) "Hierarchical and linkage analysis for the isolation of types." *Educational and Psychological Measurement* 20: 55-67.

McQUITTY, L. L. (1961) "Typal analysis." *Educational and Psychological Measurement* 21: 55-67.

McQUITTY, L. L. (1963) "Rank order typal analysis." *Educational and Psychological Measurement* 23: 55-61.

McQUITTY, L. L. (1965) "A conjunction of rank order typal analysis and item selection." *Educational and Psychological Measurement* 25: 949-961.

McRAE, D. J. (1971) "MIKCA: A FORTRAN IV Iterative *K*-Means Cluster Analysis Program." *Behavioral Science* 17: 423-424.

NEEDHAM, R. M. (1961) "The theory of clumps II." M. L. 139 (mimeographed). Cambridge: Cambridge Language Research Institute.

PARSONS, T. (1949) *The Structure of Social Action.* Glencoe, IL: Free Press.

REDFIELD, R. (1941) *The Folk Culture of the Yucatan.* Chicago: University of Chicago Press.

ROHLF, F. J., KISHPAUGH, J., and KIRK, D. (1974) *NT-SYS User's Manual.* Stony Brook: SUNY Press.

SAS Institute. (1982) *SAS User's Guide: Statistics.* New York: SAS Institute.

SAWREY, W. L., KELLER, and CONGER, J. J. (1960) "An objective method for grouping profiles by distance functions and its relation to factor analysis." *Educational and Psychological Measurement* 29: 651-673.

SIMPSON, G. G. (1961) *Principles of Animal Taxonomy.* New York: Columbia University Press.

SNEATH, P. H. A. (1957). "The application of computers to taxonomy." *Journal of General Microbiology* 17: 201-226.

SNEATH, P. H. A., and SOKAL, R. R. (1973) *Numerical Taxonomy.* San Francisco: Freeman.

SOKAL, R. R., and MICHENER, C. D. (1958) "A statistical method for evaluating systematic relationships." *University of Kansas Science Bulletin* 38: 1409-1438.

SOKAL, R. R., and SNEATH, P. H. A. (1963) *Principles of Numerical Taxonomy.* San Francisco: Freeman.

SØRENSEN, T. (1948) "A method of establishing groups of equal amplitude in plant sociology based on similarity of species content and its application to analyses of vegetation on Danish commons." *Biologiske Skrifter* 5: 1-34.

SPRADLEY, J. P. (1970) *You Owe Yourself a Drink: An Ethnography of Urban Nomads.* Boston: Little, Brown.

88

SPSS, Inc. (1988) *SPSS-X User's Guide.* 3rd edition. Chicago: SPSS, Inc.

STEPHENSON, W. (1953) *The Study of Behavior.* Chicago: University of Chicago Press.

STINCHCOMBE, A. L. (1959) "Bureaucratic and craft administration of production: A comparative study." *Administrative Science Quarterly* 4: 168-187.

STINCHCOMBE, A. L. (1968) *Constructing Social Theories.* New York: Harcourt, Brace & World.

TIRYAKIAN, E. A. (1968) "Typologies," in D. L. Sills (ed.), *International Encyclopedia of the Social Sciences,* pp. 177-186. New York: MacMillan and Free Press.

TÖNNIES, F. (1957) *Community and Society.* Translated by C. P. Loomis. Lansing: Michigan State University Press.

TRYON, R. C. (1939) *Cluster Analysis: Correlation Profile and Orthometric (Factor) Analysis for the Isolation of Unities in Mind and Personality.* Ann Arbor, MI: Edwards Brothers.

TRYON, R. C. (1955) *Identification of Social Areas by Cluster Analysis.* Berkeley: University of California Press.

TRYON, R. C., and BAILEY, D. E. (1970) *Cluster Analysis.* New York: McGraw-Hill.

TVERSKY, A. (1977) "Features of similarity." *Psychological Review* 84: 327-352.

UDY, S., Jr. (1958) "Bureaucratic elements in organizations: Some research findings." *American Sociological Review* 23: 415-418.

UDY, S., Jr. (1959) " 'Bureaucracy' and 'rationality' in Weber's organization theory: An empirical study." *American Sociological Review* 24: 791-795.

VANNEMAN, R. (1977) "The occupational composition of American classes: Results from cluster analysis." *American Journal of Sociology* 82: 783-807.

WARD, J. H., Jr. (1963) "Hierarchical grouping to optimize an objective function." *Journal of the American Statistical Association* 58: 236-244.

WARRINER, C. K. (ed.) (1979, August) "Empirical taxonomies of organizations: Problematics in their development." Presented at Roundtable Discussion, Annual Meeting of the American Sociological Association, Boston.

WEBER, M. (1947) *Theory of Social and Economic Organization.* Translated by A. R. Henderson and T. Parsons, edited by T. Parsons. Glencoe, IL: Free Press.

WEBER, M. (1949) *The Methodology of the Social Sciences.* Translated by E. A. Shils and H. A. Finch. Glencoe, IL: Free Press.

WEBER, M. (1958) "Characteristics of bureaucracy," in H. Gerth and C. W. Mills (eds.), *From Max Weber: Essays in Sociology,* pp. 196-198. New York: Galaxy Books.

WELLER, S. C., and ROMNEY, A. K. (1990) *Metric Scaling: Correspondence Analysis.* Sage University Paper series on Quantitative Applications in the Social Sciences, 07-075. Newbury Park, CA: Sage.

WILLIAMS, W. T., and LAMBERT, J. M. (1959) "Multivariate methods in plant ecology: V. Similarity analysis and information analysis." *Journal of Ecology* 54: 427-445.

WILLIAMS, W. T., LAMBERT, J. M., and LANCE, G. N. (1966) "Multivariate methods in plant ecology. V: Similarity analysis and information analysis." *Journal of Ecology* 54: 427-445.

WINCH, R. F. (1947) "Heuristic and empirical typologies: A job for factor analysis." *American Sociological Review* 12: 68-75.

WISHART, D. (1987) *CLUSTAN User Manual.* 4th edition. Edinburgh: Edinburgh University.

WRIGHT, E. O., and CHO, D. (1992) "The relative permeability of class boundaries to cross-class friendships: A comparative study of the United States, Canada, Sweden, and Norway. *American Sociological Review* 57: 85-102.

ZADEH, L. (1977) "Fuzzy sets and their application to pattern clarification and cluster analysis," in J. van Ryzin (ed.), *Classification and Clustering.* New York: Academic Press.

ZADEH, L. (1979) "Fuzzy systems theory—A framework for analysis of humanistic systems," in R. E. Cavallo (ed.), *Recent Developments in Systems Methodology for Social Science Research.* Boston: Martinus Nijhoff.

ZUBIN, J. A. (1938) "A technique for measuring likemindedness." *Journal of Abnormal and Social Psychology* 3: 508-516.

ZUBIN, J. A., FLEISS, J. L., and BURDOCK, E. I. (1963) "A method for fractionating a population into homogeneous subgroups." Unpublished manuscript.

ABOUT THE AUTHOR

KENNETH D. BAILEY is Professor of Sociology at the University of California, Los Angeles. His research interests are research methods, theory, and human ecology. He is coeditor with Bela H. Banathy and others of *Systems Inquiring,* Volume II (1985). He is author of *Methods of Social Research,* Fourth Edition (1994), which has been translated into Chinese, Italian, and Malaysian; *Social Entropy Theory* (1990); and *Sociology and the New Systems Theory* (1994). He is also the author of more than 50 articles in a wide variety of journals, including *American Sociological Review, Sociological Methodology, Sociological Methods and Research, British Journal of Sociology, Quality and Quantity,* and many others.

Printed in the United States
110953LV00003B/222/A